# One Thousand Minds Brimming

poems & art

# One Thousand

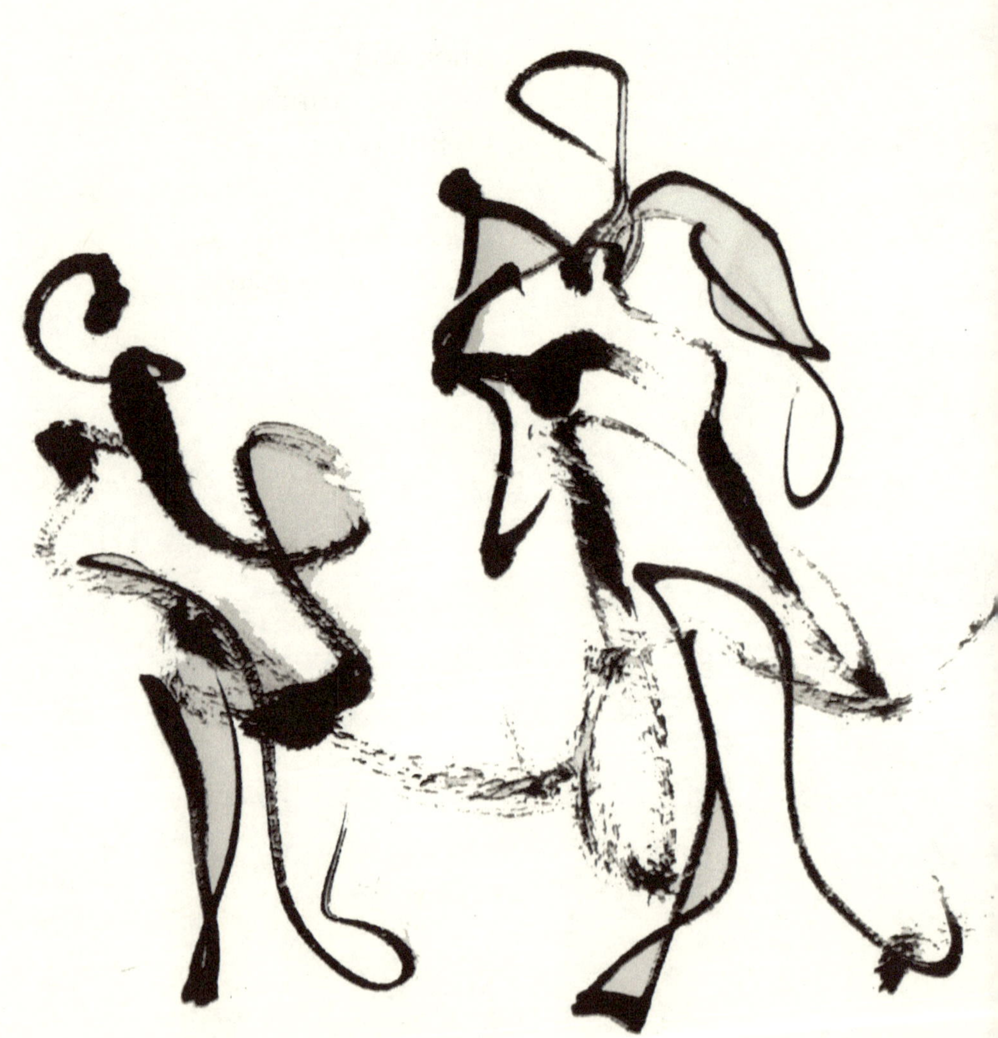

# Minds Brimming

poems & art

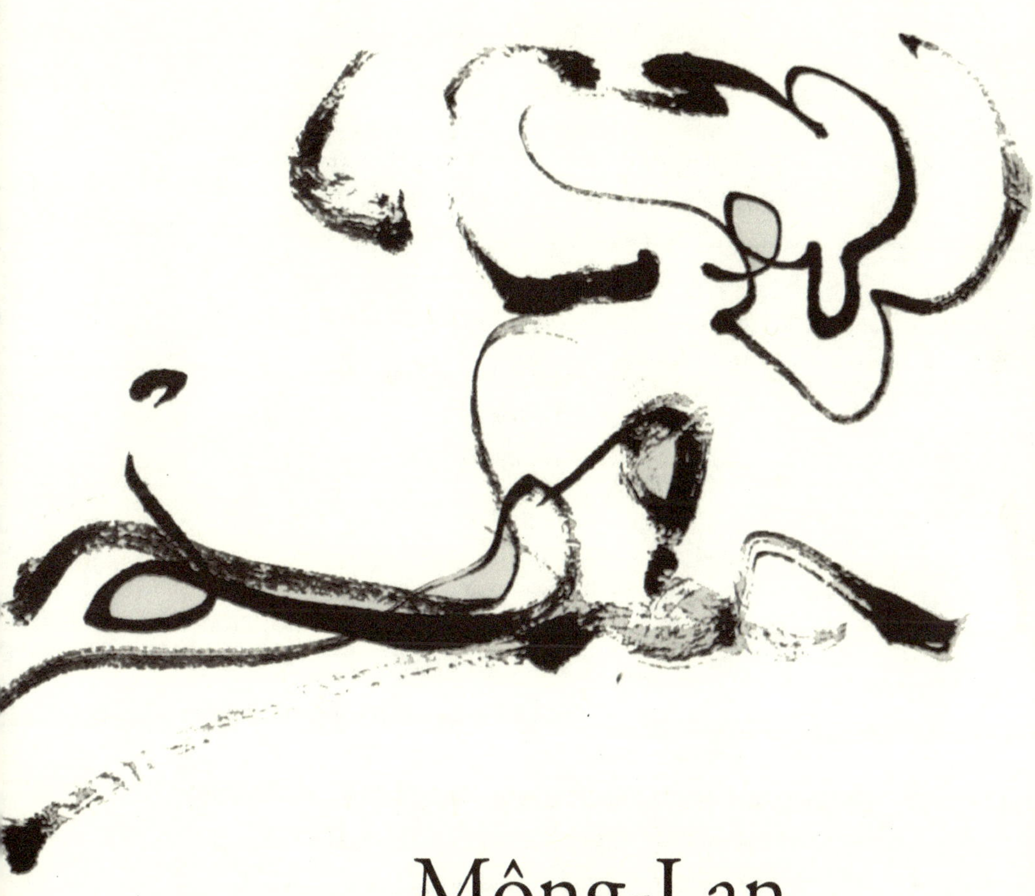

Mộng-Lan

*One Thousand Minds Brimming: poems & art*



Printed in the United States of America

ISBN-10: 0982822723

ISBN-13: 978-0-9828227-2-2

Cover photo, cover design, drawings and paintings by Mộng-Lan

Cover photos, front: "Two School Girls on Bicycle in Saigon," 2007.

Back: "Galveston Beach Horizon," 2012.

Published by Valiant Press

PO Box 2771

Sugar Land, Texas 77487

Other Books by Mộng-Lan

www.monglan.com

*Song of the Cicadas* (Juniper Prize)

*Why is the Edge Always Windy?*

*Tango, Tangoing: Poems & Art*

*Tango, Tangueando: Poemas & Dibujos* (bilingual Spanish-English edition)

*Love Poem to Tofu & Other Poems* (poetry & calligraphic art, chapbook)

*Force of the Heart: Tango, Art* (drawings, paintings, a poem)

*Love Poem to Ginger & Other Poems* (poetry & calligraphic art, chapbook)

for my loved ones

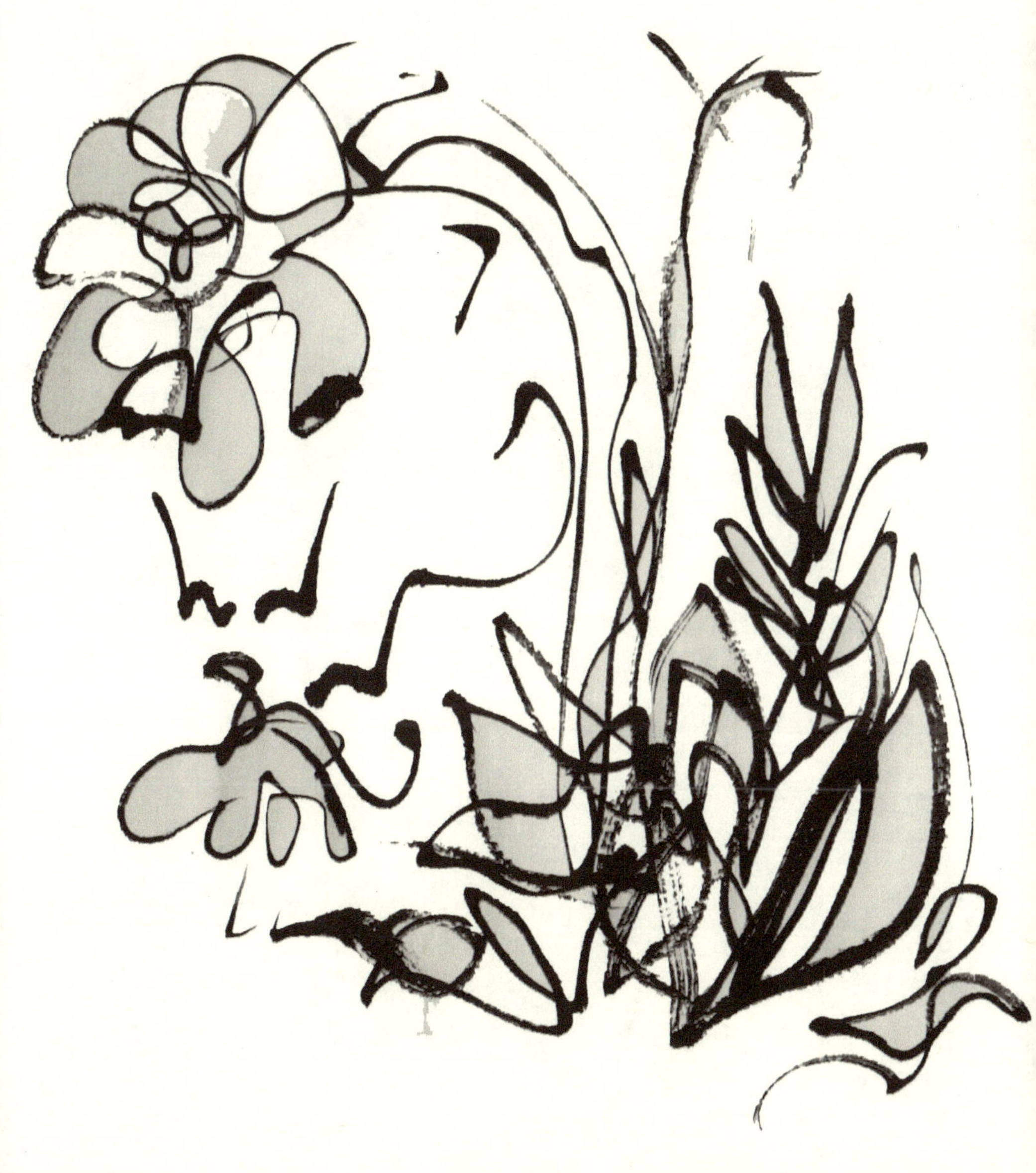

# CONTENTS

**One Thousand Minds Brimming**



**Hallucination with Clay**



**Love Poems II**

**Smoky Cities, Pigeons' Wings**

# ACKNOWLEDGEMENTS

Deep appreciation to all of my family and friends throughout the world who have inspired me, supported me, shared your wisdom, your loving friendship and kindness through the years. Special thanks to my mother Dr. Bui Nhu, my sister Dr. Rose Pham, Dr. Joe Arden, Dr. David Shapiro, Ravi Shankar, Dr. Kirk Patterson, Ken Fields, and Pablo Di Lauro.

Grateful acknowledgements to the editors of the following journals and literary magazines where my poems first appeared:

*Asian American Literary Review*, "Love poem to Nước Mắm"; "Love poem to Lemons"; "Love poem to Leeks"; "The Bodywasher"

*The Antioch Review*, "Bangkok [neon lights]"

*Artful Dodge*, "love poem to thick rice noodles"

*Bayou*, "Love Poem to Cherry Blossoms"

*BN Magazine*, "Straw Village, Humid Night"

*Cerise Press*, "Love Poem to Soto," www.cerisepress.com

*Cimarron Review*, "Love Poem to Shitake Mushroom," "Love Poem to Broccoli," "Love Poem to Green Tea"

*Colorado Review*, "Love Poem to Spinach"

*Constellation*, "Leblon-Ipanema-Copacabana"; "Mountain Mysticism"

*Da Mau*, "Love Poem to Bánh Cuốn," "Love Poem to Bún Riêu," "Love Poem to Spinach," www.damau.org

*Drunken Boat*, "Sentient Figure"; "Memory a distinct black hole" (forthcoming) www.drunkenboat.com

*ISLE*, "Desert Mysticism" and "The Imperial Palace, Tokyo"

*Kenyon Review*, "Bangkok: City Streets"; "Bangkok: Royalty"

*Nha Magazine*, "Love Poem to Café au Lait"; "Love Poem to Red Chili Peppers"

*Nhip Song*, "A Bamboo Stick;" "Love Poem to Tofu"

*North American Review*, "Love Poem to Phở" and "Flight"

*Pleiades*, "A Bird of Laughing Feathers"

*Seattle Review*, "Upon Seeing Marcel Marceau"; "Seoul Snow"

*Seneca Review*, "Proof"

*World Literature Today*, "Love Poem to Garlic"; "Love Poem to Onion"; "Love Poem to Ginger"; "Love Poem to Basil"

# BAMBOO KNIFE

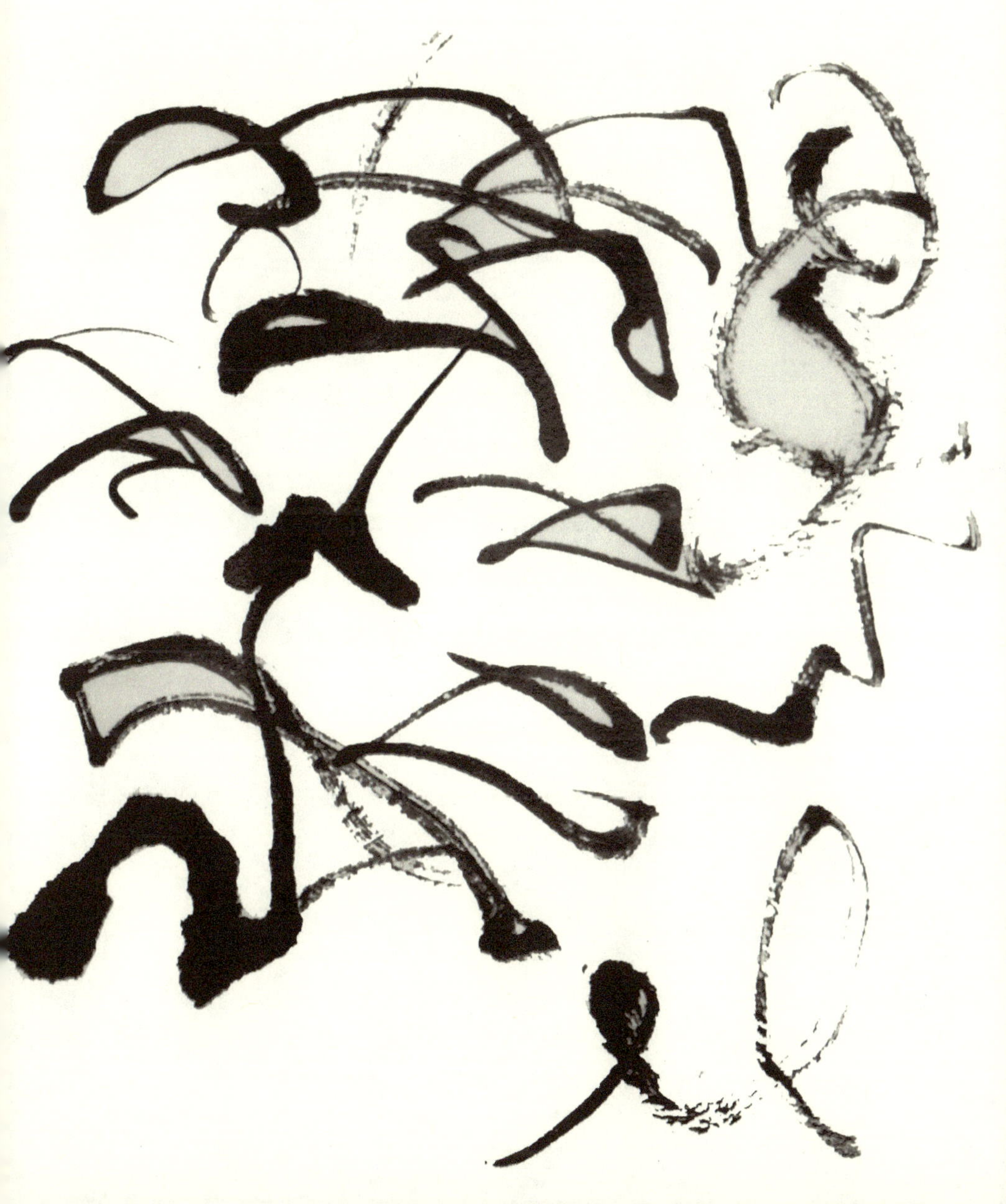

## Proof

in this city where you do not live
you were born
the city itself no longer exists on a map
of Vietnam
the street on which you were
born does not exist
for its name has changed
if you had continued
to exist here  if you had stayed after war's end
now 30 yrs later you would be walking down the street talking
joking philosophizing suffering with friends
you would be a closed-eyed bicycle-motor-riding adult
married with children

the house where you lived         the first five years
of your life was seized
& therefore does not exist
as you knew it
it sits on a street whose name has changed
no longer recognizable

your grandparent's house
also appropriated
now people live there eating making love defecating

spinning new lives for themselves from the walls

of your past

in the city where you were born

you do not now exist because the city

no longer exists

the grandparents whom you met

in your imagination

& memory did exist

& gave birth to your parents

who exist in a different country & plane altogether

not in this city

of faint turquoise   limestone   whiteness &   charcoal

of your imagination

two handfuls of cities

changed names through wars or revolutions

the hospital where you were born still remains

*that* exists & still keeps

its name   Hôpital Saint-Paul

does that prove anything?

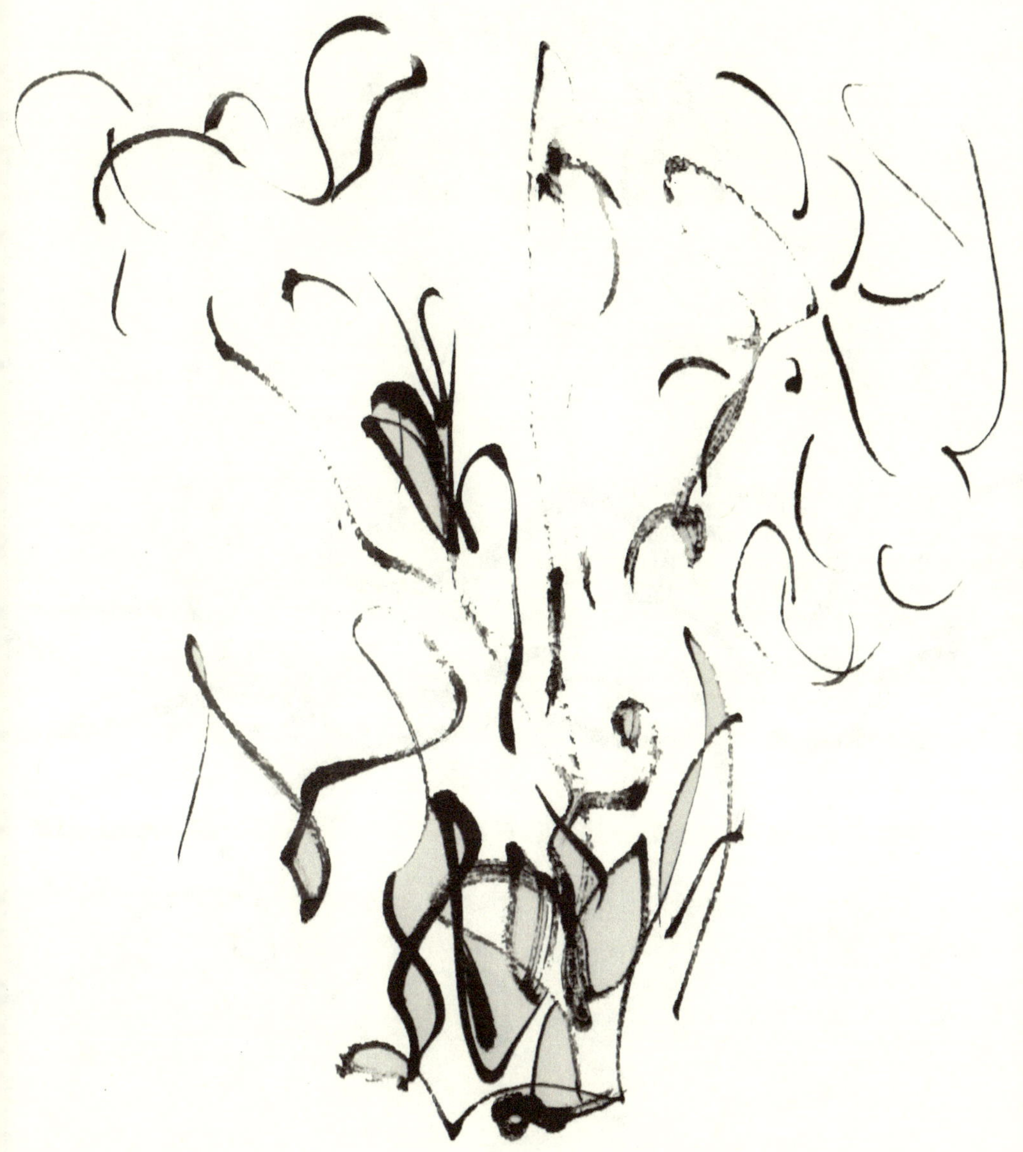

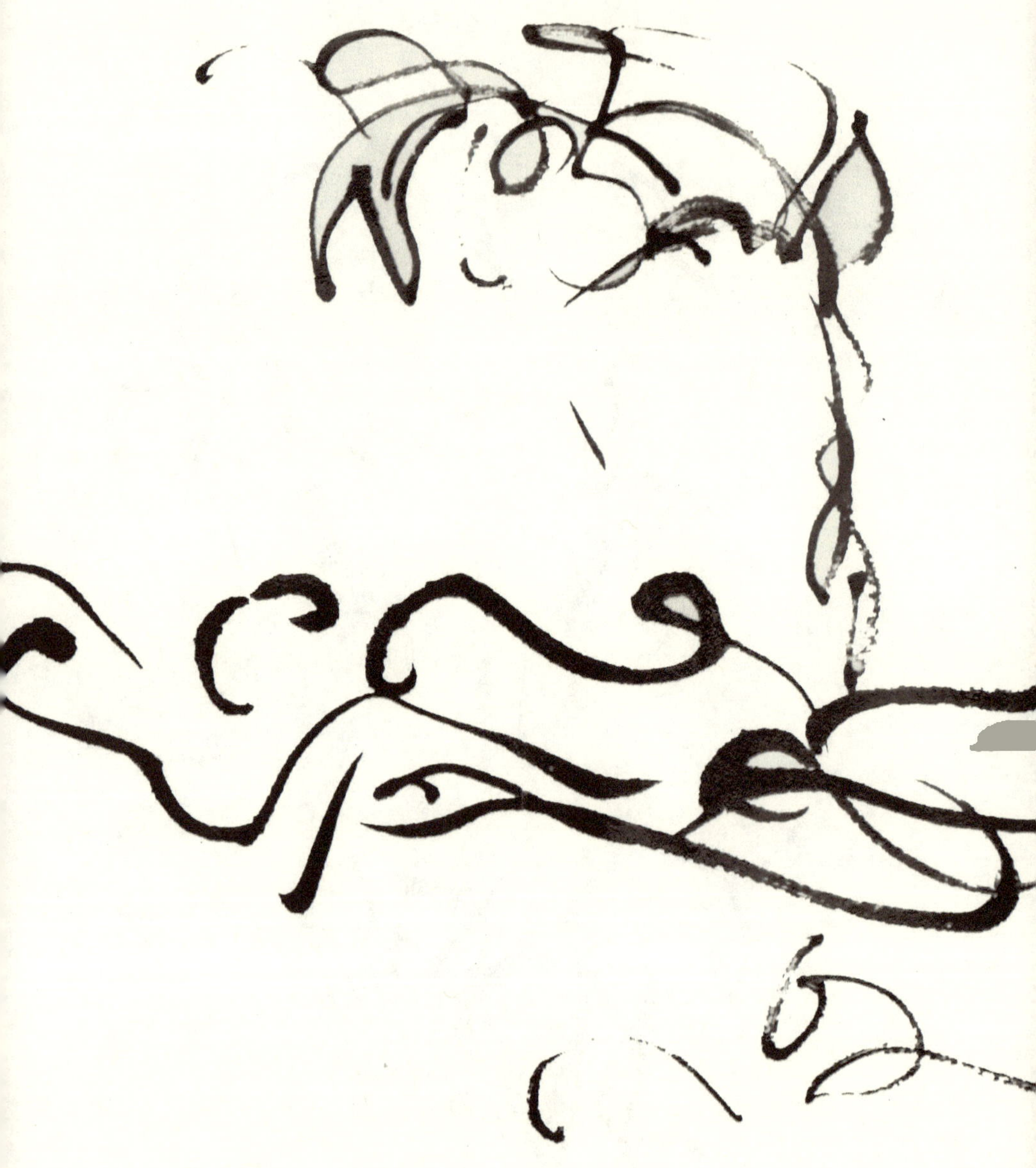

## A Bamboo Knife

1

to cut the umbilical cord

but what to cut the hysteria    the mania  the
melancholia?

Great Grandmother    born December 7, 1878
died June 17, 1962
Hà Đông    North Vietnam

a spoon to carve out the child    from rice & malaria
a bag of bones to sink the body
a scythe to kill someone with
a map of the moon to go thereafter

2

from each birth    bloodletting
each baby alive to this world
for a few days    then returned to the ether
world    with
only
a name

only *one* survived

3

five fetuses
five years
of being bloated five years
of carrying

the midwife cut each umbilical cord with bamboo
each time

the baby turned porcelain blue stopped breathing
after a few days
infection tetanus it was said

only one was strong enough to survive
infancy

my body
could not take the grief
trembling crying i buried each blue
child in the cemetery
i was loud brash given to fits
& sadness

4

i raised my only child to utter pristineness
as i could
although all around us was unrest  always  blackness
a magnetic current   of wasps

he learned to treat the illnesses of others
in the village        married and had children himself

the years were punctuated with increasing violence

uncertainty

5

*1954*

my only child  his wife  my grandchildren    they have all
left

not given me word
while sleeping  i dream of emptiness    an empty egg

an uninhabited coffin
when i wake up
they are all gone

## 6

do they blame me for having a tongue?

perhaps they wanted to cut

my tongue

where have they gone?

even the spirits don't tell me

i pull out my hair    scream

for the ancestors  anybody
to hear

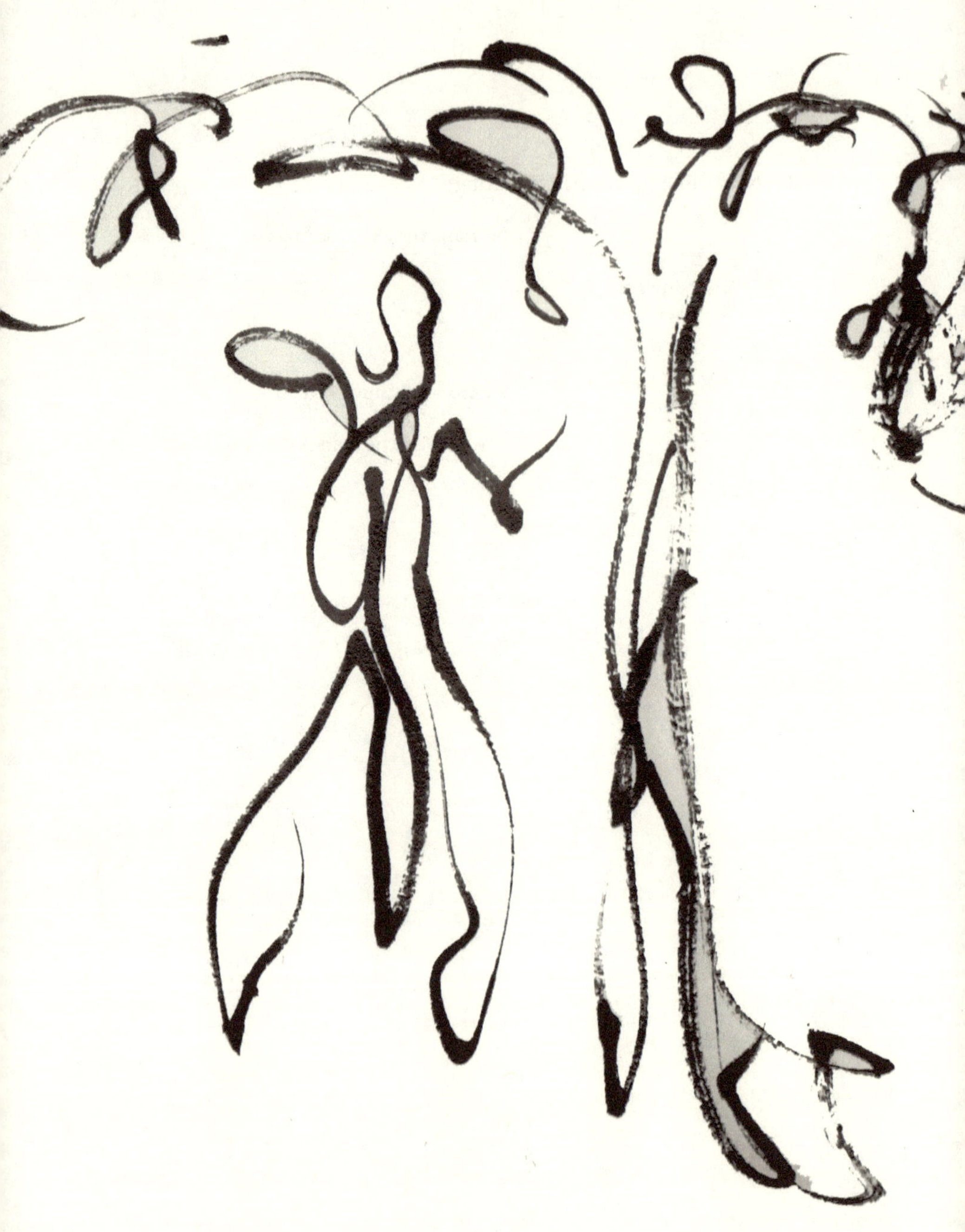

7

the soldiers come    the Việt  Cộng    they seize my house
take my land    take all my possessions
consign me to a tree behind my house

make me eat dirt

thank Buddha
i am so old   they leave my shriveled sex alone

but they chew
my tongue        then    spit it out

# Straw Village Humid Night

1

*a young woman 14    Bình An village   1947*

what i remember    taunting sweet rain

i can't peel the humidity off
a few seconds of being outdoors
mosquitoes bite me   mercilessly

i sip the thick air
heat so high i drown in it daily

some nights after working  i lay awake
& dream of my future husband

our house we built from straw
the fields & clay
from  river banks
we grow rice  *rau muống*  raise chickens
leeches suck
my ankles
while i tend
the lilting  rice shoots

## 2

when the French troops burst
into our house at dusk  my skin reacts an unbearable
stinging  my mind explodes

brutality & lust in their eyes
frantically i run for
my life to the next village
*fearing rape more than*
*death*

my father  a school principal
speaks
*nous ne sommes pas de genres*
*militaires  nous ne combattons pas*

they don't touch him  perhaps  for his white hair
perhaps for his French

the soldiers (French sympathizers Africans
Vietnamese)  brusquely
move & destroy  barbarity
flickering in their eyes

3

they haul my brothers to the base    pour
water
into their moth
mouths

pulling them by the hairstrings
my brothers'
jerking heads
mouths dumb
swallow the suffocating water

the soldiers kick
their bloated stomachs

old tires

4

after my brothers trek
back home we destroy our house &
move away from barbarity
to Hà Nội the city *civilisation*

i hear that they killed my uncles
*how* i do not know

we harbor in Hà Nội for several years
until the newspapers say
that the communists
will take the North

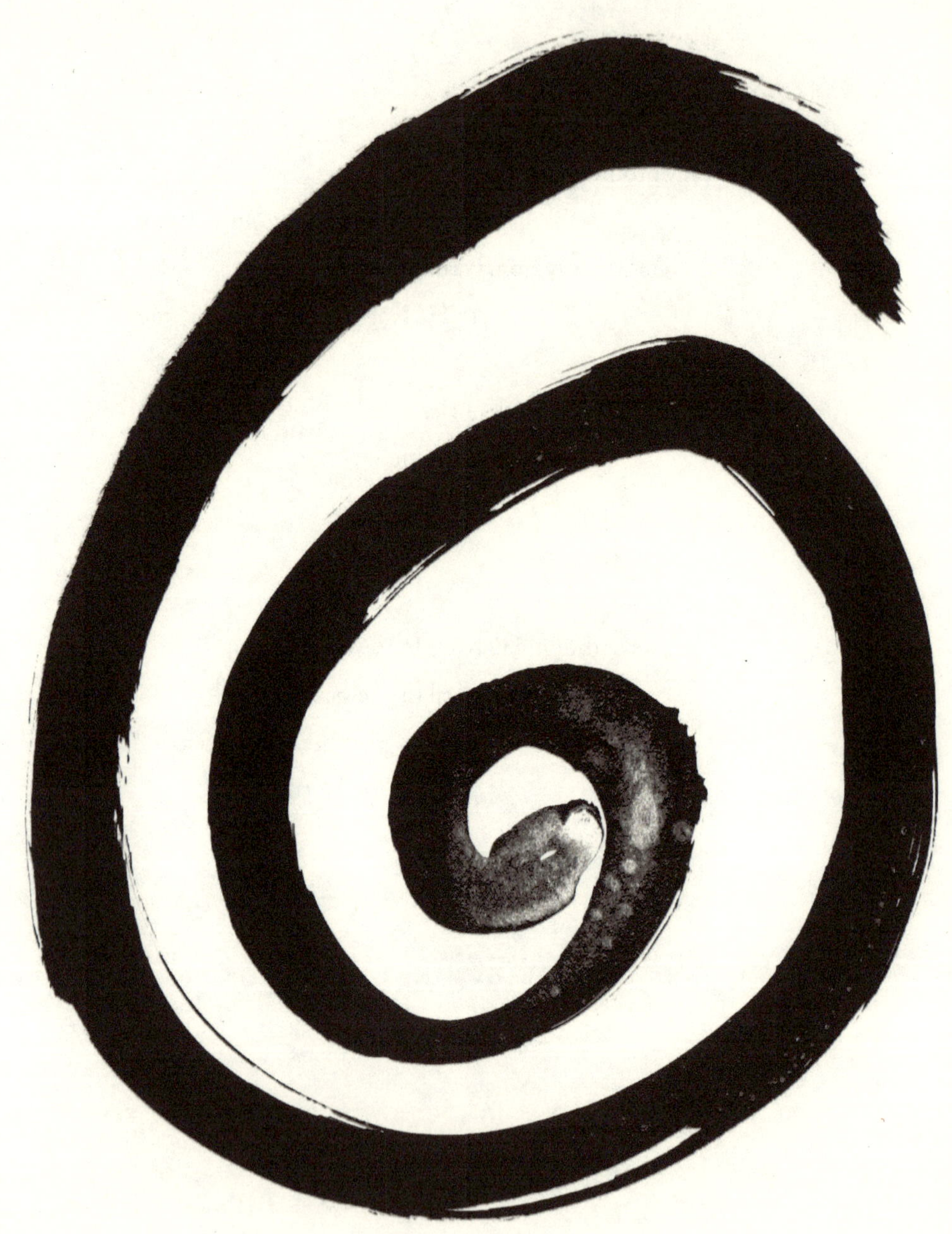

# Memory a distinct black hole

*1954, Hà Nội*
Mother doesn't know where to piss or shit

i her only son tie her hands to the papaya tree in the backyard
when she falls into her sputtering fits

afterwards when the Việt Cộng come we hear that she's delirious
shouting mouth uncontrollable like the cicadas' drone
escape for us would've been impossible

the police the Việt Cộng after us like
fire ants

she would've told the neighbors everybody
had my mother known of our plans

§

the radio blares *Hồ Chí Minh will take the North*

i tell myself to let go let go of everything let go so we can go forward
the house my parents our lands
our memories

death's drone wakes me up

thunder on trembling tin roof

the hum of never ending bullets through our pupils

searches at point blank
continuous shooting pulses

corpuscles of ammunition in their trained-to-kill blood

bubbles of gunshot in the mouth

sulfur swirling

a black hole of memory where everything

is re-membered

# Night the high seas

1

March 2000

a boat vessel to another life

when we escape:

first to a dark island then to a larger boat

about 25 five of us board a dark vessel

with provisions for several days

angel dust line our clothes

## 2

after 3 days on the high seas
we see a ship from afar suddenly Thai pirates descend
like hungry bats rodents vultures with endless
claws & beaks
a pirate wields a knife jumps on my brother

a pirate jumps my legs pry them open a knife inserted into

the impact of the world

how many pirates violate me
i stop counting i do not understand their fierceness
such hatred might of skin
blood & brutal
desire

3

the high seas brew black

unpredictable yet compulsory death

the rocking boat which does not give

the blue of the sea defiled
the purity of the sea shaken

in mid-air a pirate struggles forces my brother
overboard

suddenly no more time

the pirates grasp everything: our oars motor sails jewelry & gold
our food
my brother
my body
our lives to come

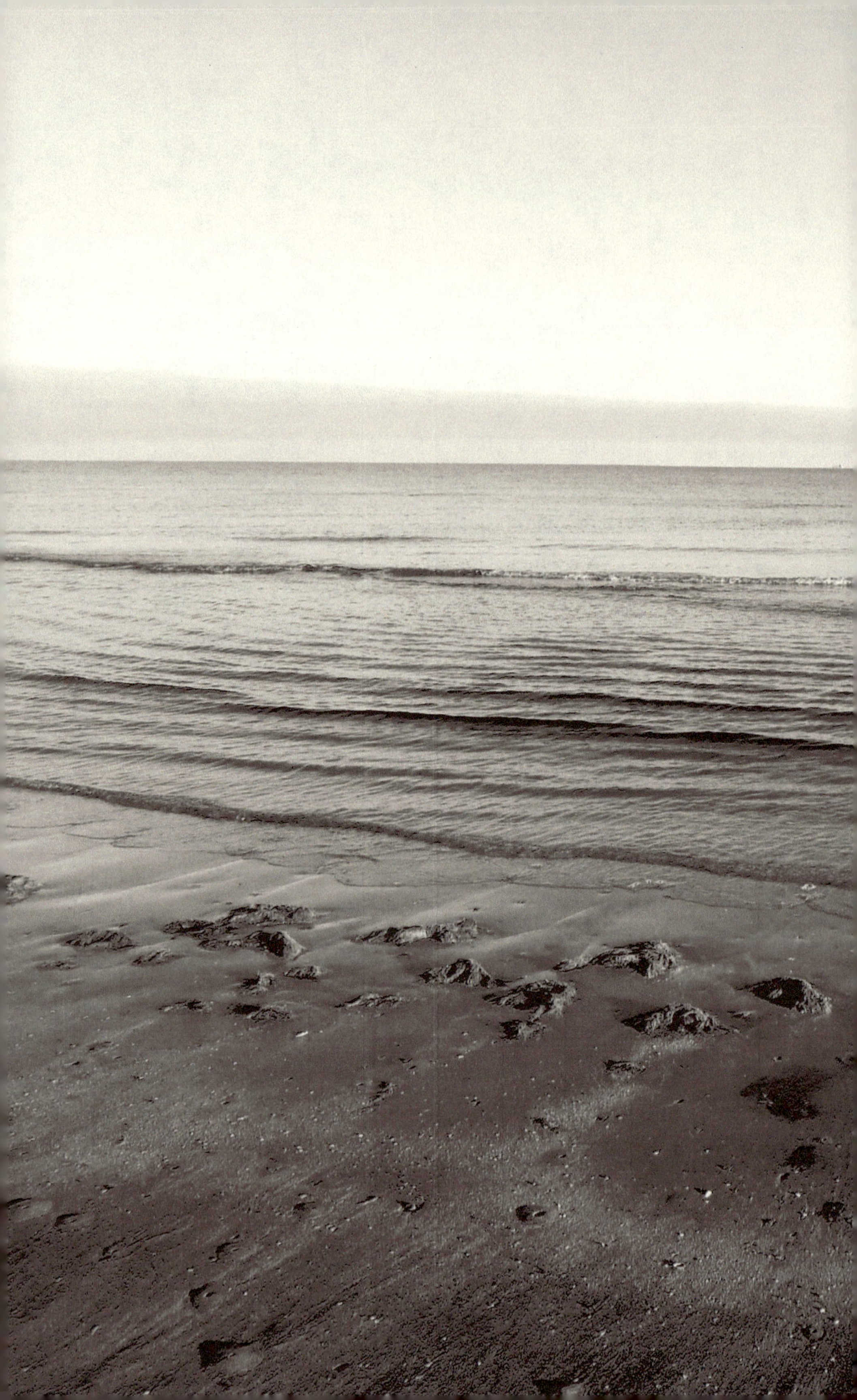

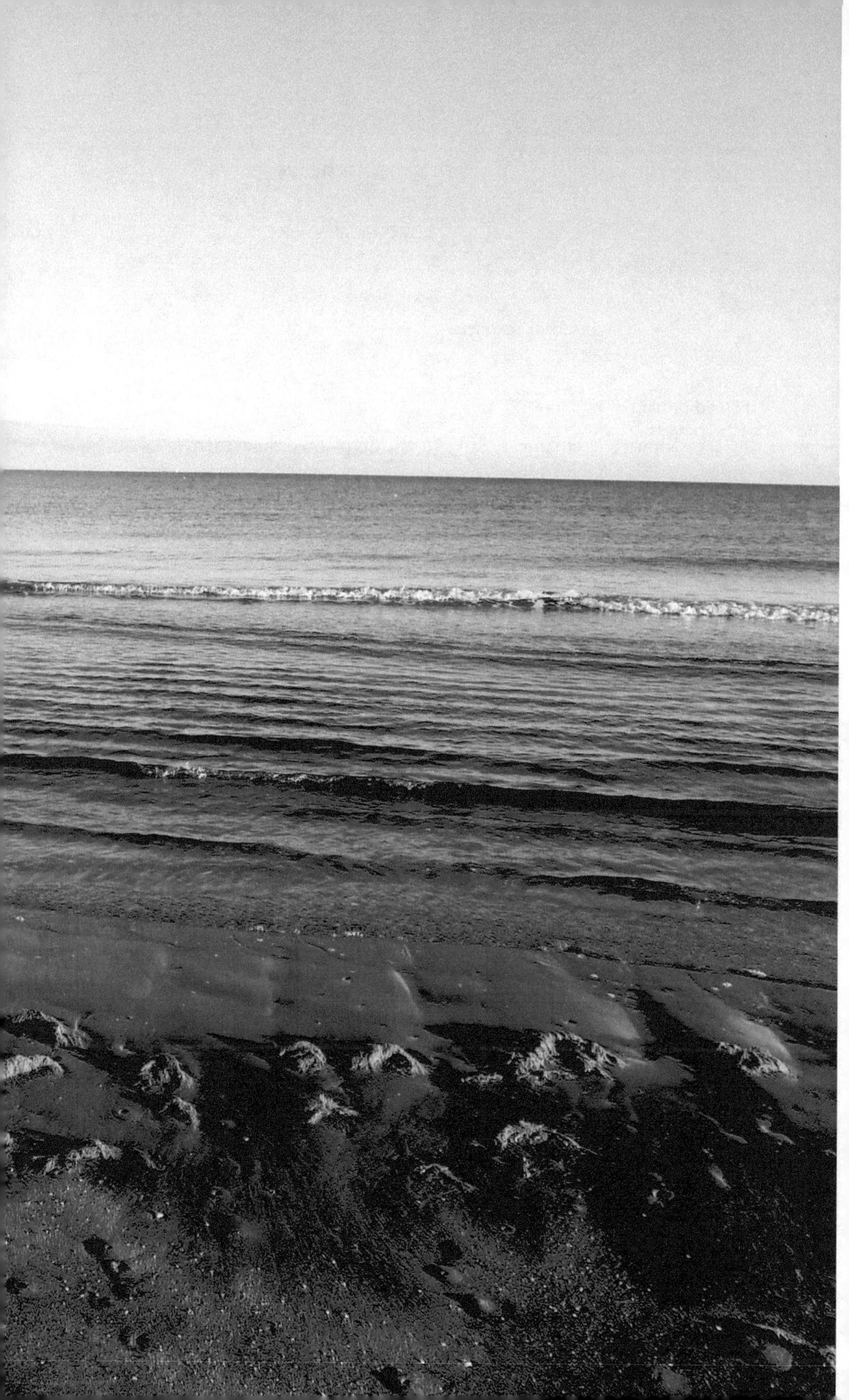

## Shrapnel in heart

internal   external

instead of fruit
Khmers  Vietnamese  &  Americans planted them there
landmines
in the rumbling earth
limbless bodies   Pol Pot reaped death as the fruit of life

now  so many walk without legs
prostheses   plastic  stumps   living around lakes
in Phnom Penh
dust rises in
havoc
children like the elderly   beg
names written on old skin

especially   forget they are there

2

robed with sickness    jobless
they sleep around the lake with babies
in their arms
the dust heat & sweat their blanket

plastic sandals littered around the lake
for their one remaining foot

3

many years after the war
shrapnel still lurk in his flesh: five pieces in arm
two in his head                two in lungs

one in the heart

# LOVE POEMS I

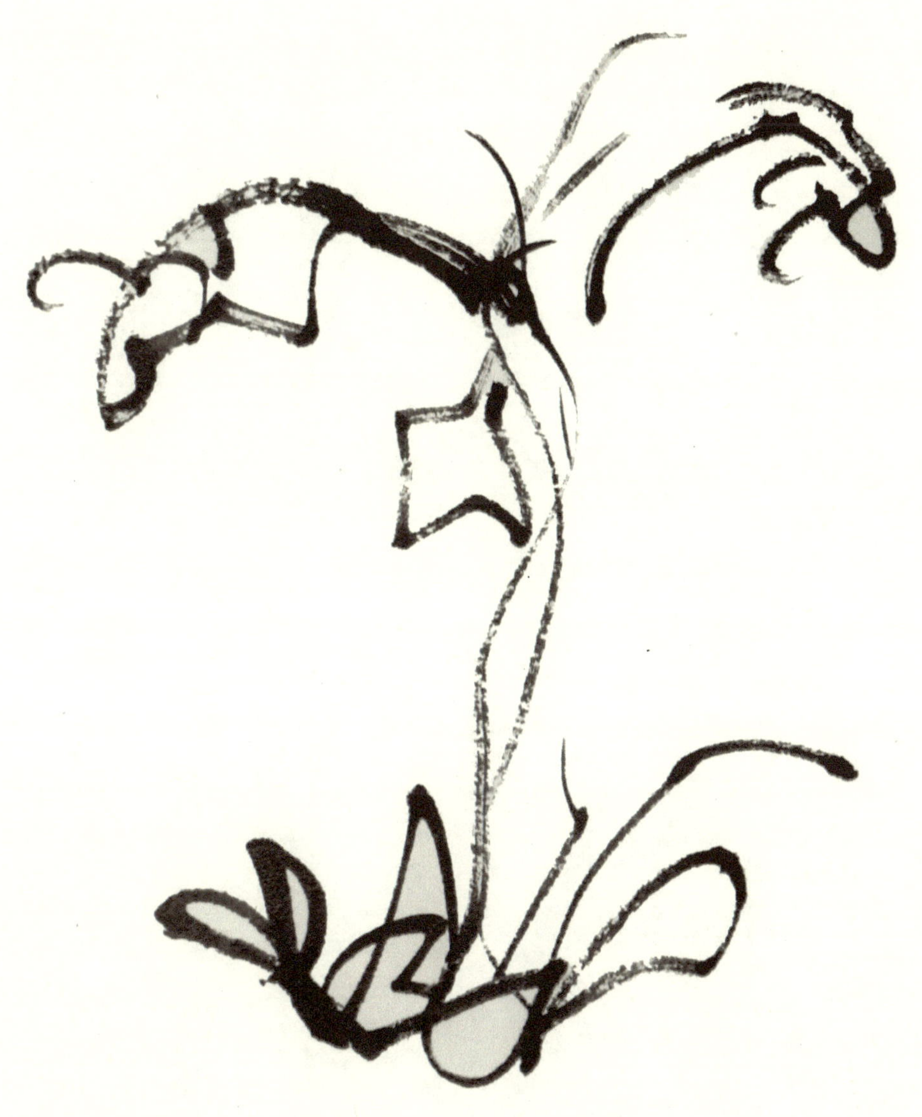

# Love Poem to Tofu

everyday i open you up
with a knife slice you in half boil eat you

O how i need you warm creamy-white loaded with vegetable protein
how can i live
without your textured taste?
i don't even remember
when we first met: it must have been
in Sài Gòn in a soup dish my mother made with tomatoes
& a solitary
flaming egg
for many years i knew you made in California not as
good as in Vietnam but now in Tokyo
you once again
become divine

you are exquisite plain dipped in soy sauce or *nước mắm*
with a bit of lemon
& cayenne pepper

varieties of you i love silken firm braised
tofu i feast upon you

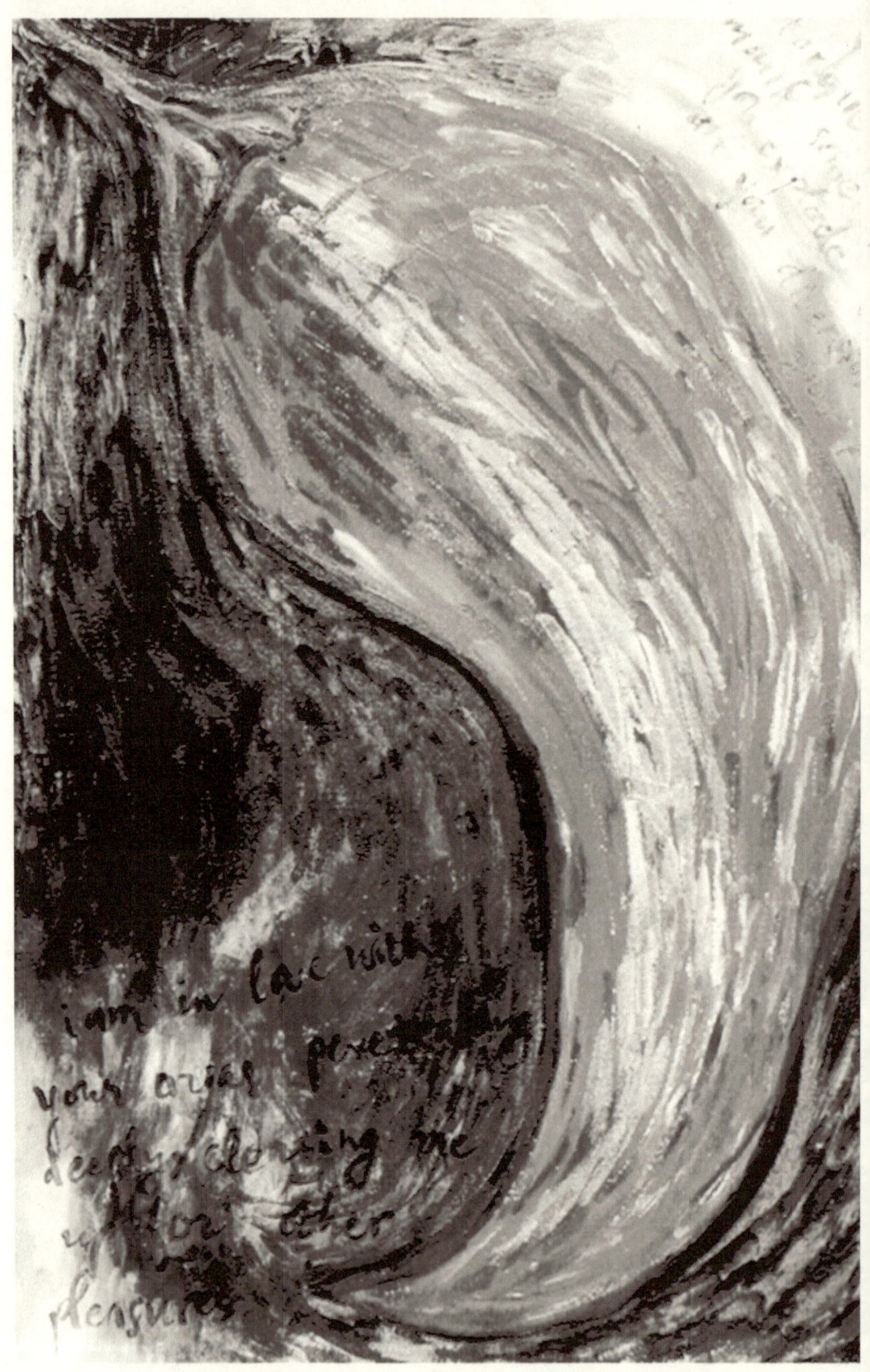

## Love Poem to Red Chili Peppers

your red hot tongue
slips into my mouth    sometimes
unknowingly    you explode with each bite
all your diversions & fireworks    your petulant sting

i can't adequately extol you
for you are a paradox    your unassuming tongue brings terror
to most people    but to me brings
ecstasy.
where did you receive all your powers?
perhaps from the ubiquitous Sun
you pack in her rays

i am in love with your arias    penetrating deeply
clearing me up for other pleasures

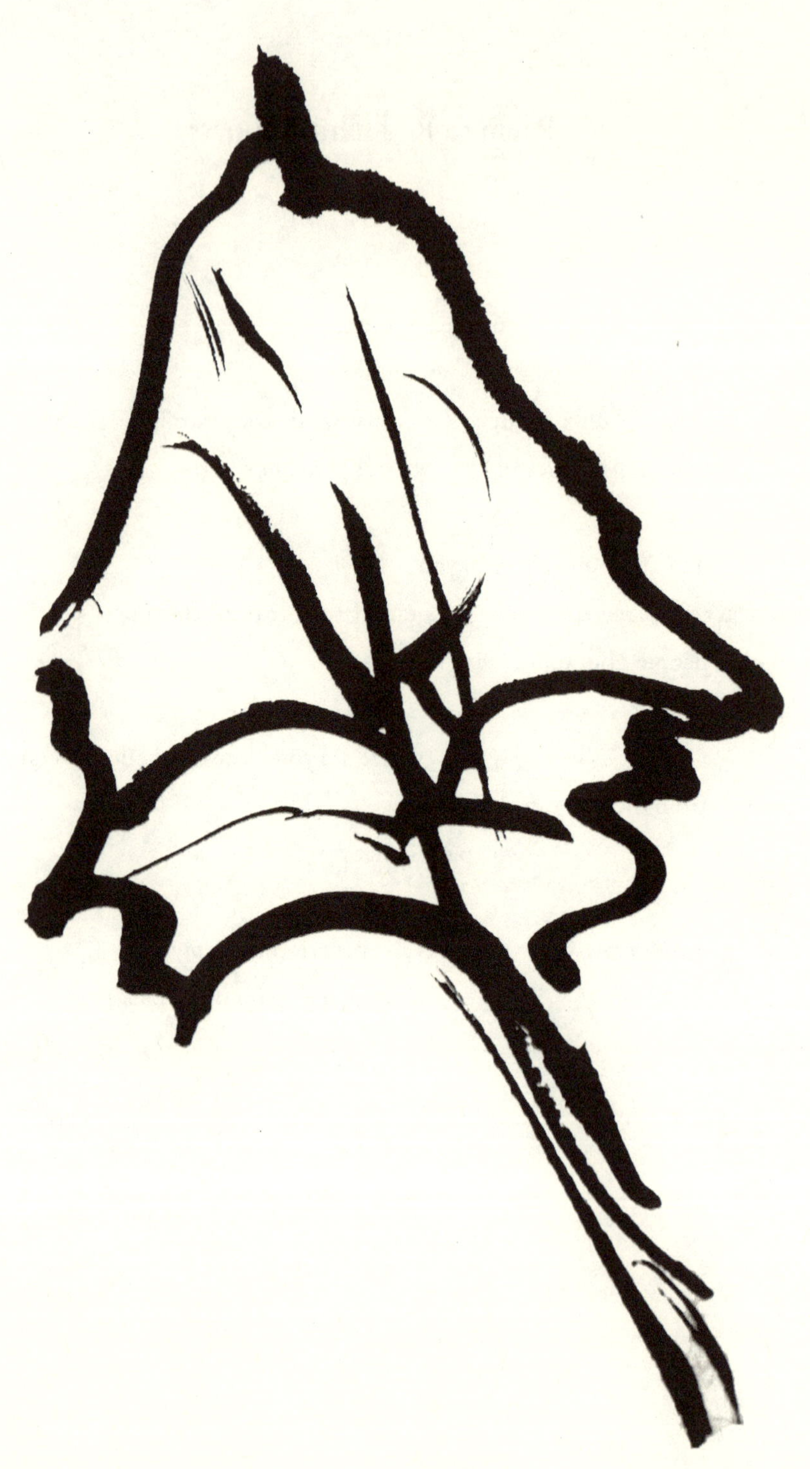

## Love Poem to Spinach

your vulgar name is "Spinach" but your
glorious Latinate name is *Spinacia Oleracea*
of the goosefoot family

your large   dark-green juicy   edible leaves are beacons
sending tremors through my body

am i masochistic?  loving you that most hate—

i took to liking you immediately
then the love came later    stronger

i find you absolutely necessary:  your stalks & leaves full of iron

you are luscious
sweet
divine
you empower anyone
who eats you
close to your original glory
is how i want you

# Love Poem to *Bánh Cuốn*

i learned to make you once   & you were difficult
nothing worth it is easy

when i was young   in Sài Gòn & in little Saigons in America
i ate you with minced pork
mushrooms prawn
you are delicate   white layers of flimsy rice film   like white wings
ready to fly
wherever the eater wishes
a special treat   we devoured you on Sunday
mornings as if there was nothing
left on earth
nothing to do   no yearning
but being with family
nothing to wish for   but luxuriating
in the fish sauce
spiked with chili peppers and lemons
the days of youth

now   when i find you   i eat you vegetarian style   without meat
with a concoction of soy sauce   lemon   & chili peppers
i linger over your melting body
in my mouth   take your labia   &
swallow

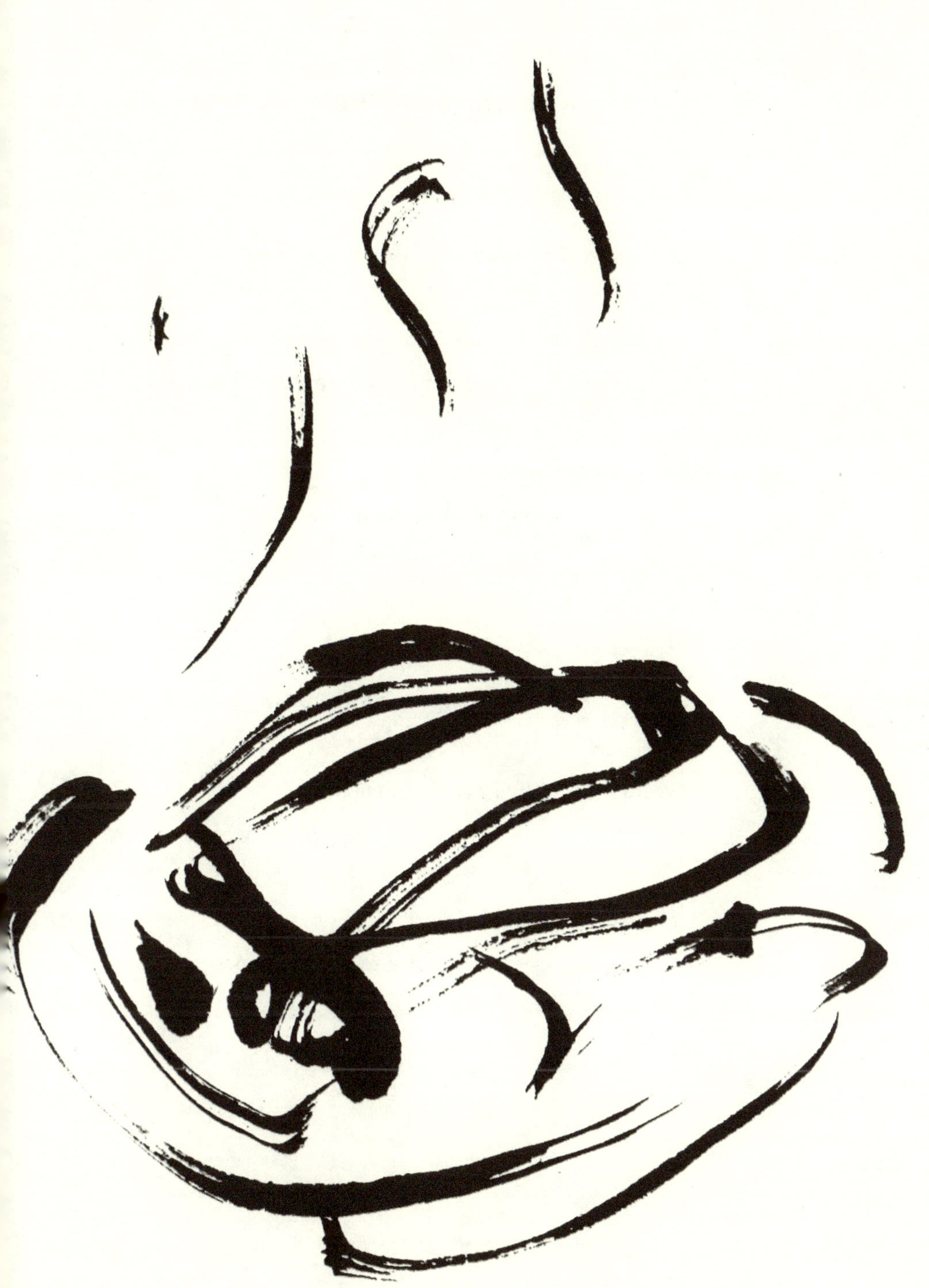

## Love Poem to *Bún Riêu*

a bowl of *bún riêu*     eaten at *Chợ Lớn*

rice vermicelli in a rich broth of tomatoes shrimp & crabmeat
eating my way into memory a moth
i remember
every delicious sliver of rice vermicelli
every succulent dumpling
every slurp

my lost city
under broth and soup

cousins fighting  dying at sea  or far away
escaping one's country

loss is all-encompassing
down to the last drop

## Love Poem to Thick Rice Noodles

O your thick body  luscious as a pillow
in base of tomato & shrimp
my tongue glides over your cellophane

under large blue umbrellas
in Sài Gòn  i eat you
with crabmeat delicate & chewy
while the youths with AK guns strapped
over their shoulders  motorcycles thundering on

in East Palo Alto  i eat you
in a sautéed dish with garlic onions tofu & leek

while hearing gun shots
police sires  ambulances
plangent trucks passing in front of my house

## Love Poem to Shitake

who are you, really?
you are so elusive    like Pluto the moon

lunar disked
you were there
ready to greet me early
in the world

my first experience
of you    though from desiccated form
were filling enough
but in Japan   i discovered you
fresh
as the day is plump    juicy
& whole
fighting cancer   building bones
cleaning blood    you make me stronger
than i would be

luscious
fungus  you are sweet
unapologetic

secretly growing in the enigmatic dark

is where you get your power

exuding confidence

in fried rice soups stir fries spring rolls

in everything i surrender

to you my utmost care

preparing you for the meal

to you i surrender

your delicate umber

stout umbrellas

thick protective legs

yes you are physically obtuse

but love is in the mouth

not in the eyes

## Love Poem to Broccoli

insensate   you are   bringing me over
like this
your dominant curlicues
are green   placid
your crunch soothing to the spine

cancer-fighting
your scintillating frilly-green dresses
little heads blooming   undress before me

how delicious you are
how full of potassium!
spirited
you are erect   muscular
bunchy with blossoms   little promises waiting
to be fulfilled

## Love Poem to *Phở*

yes, i am guilty

i am not a good Buddhist vegetarian
when in Sài Gòn or Hà Nội, i sometimes sneak bowls of you
from the vendor
down the street    for fifty cents or less
always without meat    bowls of *phở* clear fatless broth
of chicken or beef

i sneak bowls of you past my other moral self
a secret sin  to remind me of days without pressure

without animal flesh i slurp you down
only the perfume of you

i slurp you
as Asians are wont to do  making noise to make
the taste sweeter
i slurp you with fresh
cilantro  lemon  mint leaves  dragon *phở* leaves
i slurp you with hot chili peppers tingling the tongue

fresh green peppers of memory penetrating
the palate

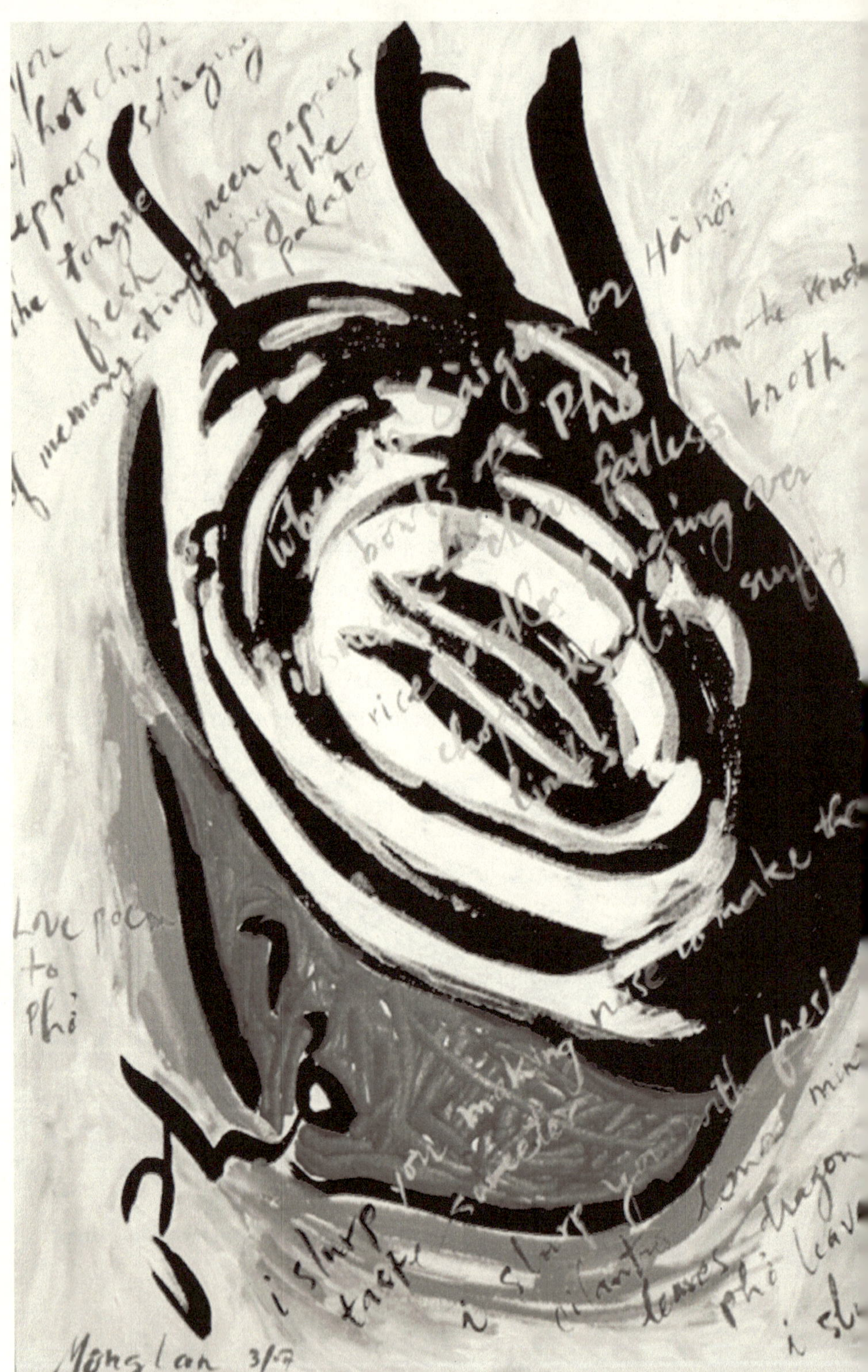
Love poem
to
Phở
Mộng Lan 3/07

rice noodles    hanging over chopsticks  ubiquitous legs

the Japanese say you have  "a simple elegant taste"
Vietnamese know you are never to be colonized

at home  i make you with a vegetable broth
rice noodles  & vegetables

your broth   transparent
humble

# One Thousand Minds Brimming

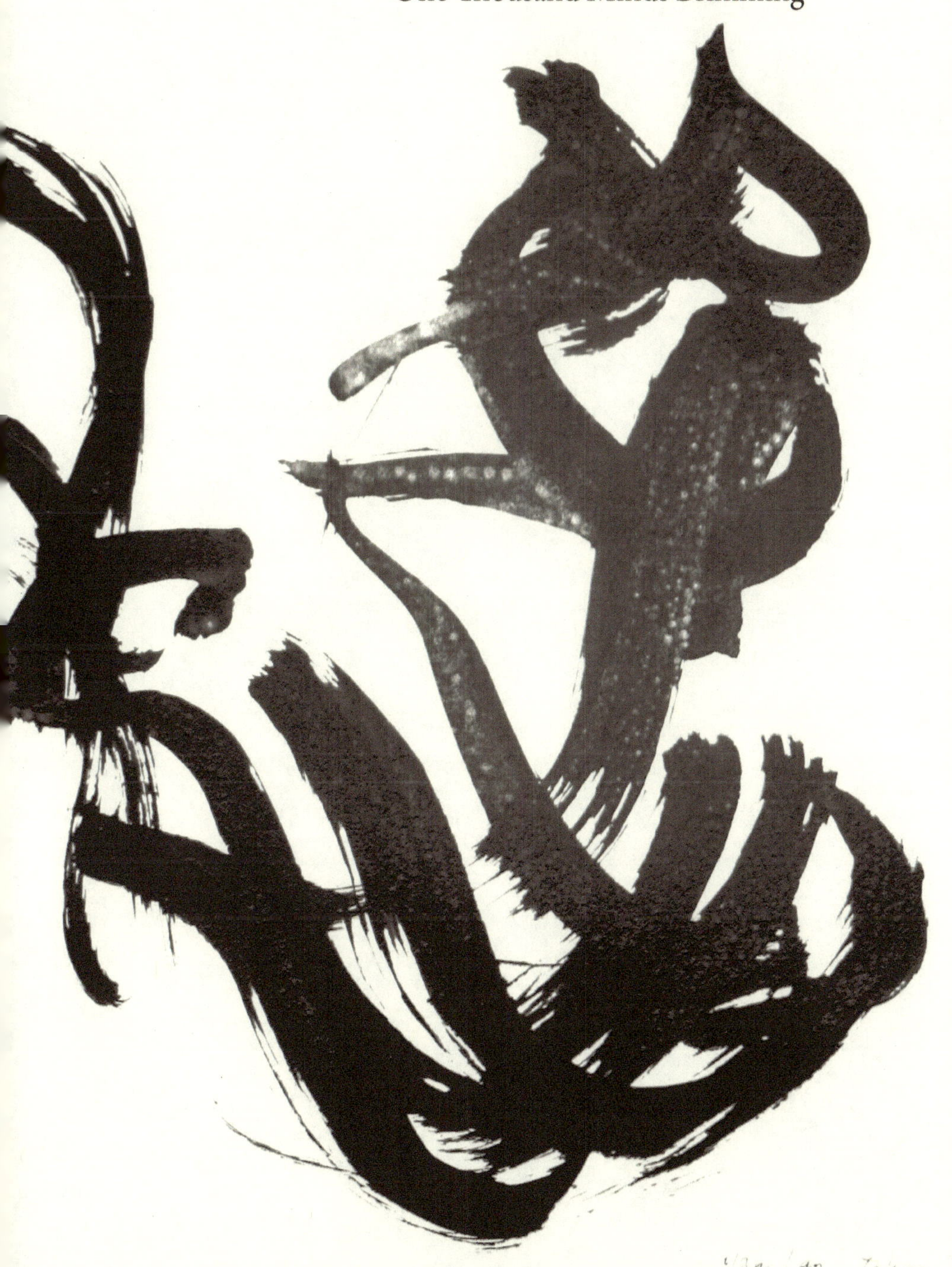

## Bangkok: City Streets

The silk maker walked

into the forest & never returned

§

Making love to you natural clean

Did you think to bring happiness?

Morning's burgeoning mass—

how rare it is to see the light of a thousand

minds brimming

Mad *tuk tuks* roaring swerving

wildly in pitch to long tailed boats on

*Chao Phraya* River River of Kings

Emaciated cats

babies all of them elusively slink

Elephants walk

pavements

begging

for sugarcane &

the men riding them

§

Walk on *Charoen Krung* Road

Machinery of noise as if in a vault   cars running
up your nervous system   your veins   echo of
            grime echo of industry clamoring up buildings
                        noises metallic   & clanking
                                    rubbing against each other

                        In the vortex young men walk
        proud   erect   youthful

# Bangkok: Royalty

O incongruous city!   Bangkok roars
with a bang!

Disco Elephants—O king of the forest

You walk with feet pounding
city cement   the world's weight on you   beggars
the destitute

§

Ogling taxi drivers   loud-mouthed gap-toothed buildings
3 scrawny dogs sleeping in street crevices
a dog on corner   sleeping on noise & depravity

3 lonely dogs on the streets   crooning their loves
Boats tug a V in the water
a Chinese spy angles in for a joke

§

A taxi driver with bad energy drunk
behind the wheel
O bustling river

& the glass-eyed King
peering unfathomable from colossal framed portraits
next to his queen
at the swarm of people

## Bangkok: River

"the bandits' muzzle flash singed
your jet black hair"

Christmas Eve lepered people
sit on Bangkok boulevards nubs for hands
eyes smeared into flesh
barely with feet
begging
Multifarious colored lights cheesy yuletide ornaments
overflow the streets

Girls & women abound beautiful girls women
selling themselves cheap

§

From his traditional Thai house of old teak the American silk maker
walked into the forest & did not return

§

O city of forever   stretching beyond your years

O river of commerce   *Chao Phraya* of ten thousand barges   nosing
down the river aquiline fashion

Meditating on this river more than a thousand years

long tailed boats in perfect splendor   bright reds
blues   oranges

& sky trains criss-crossing the heavens

Pyramids of gold rise
from the shores of the river's
stirrings

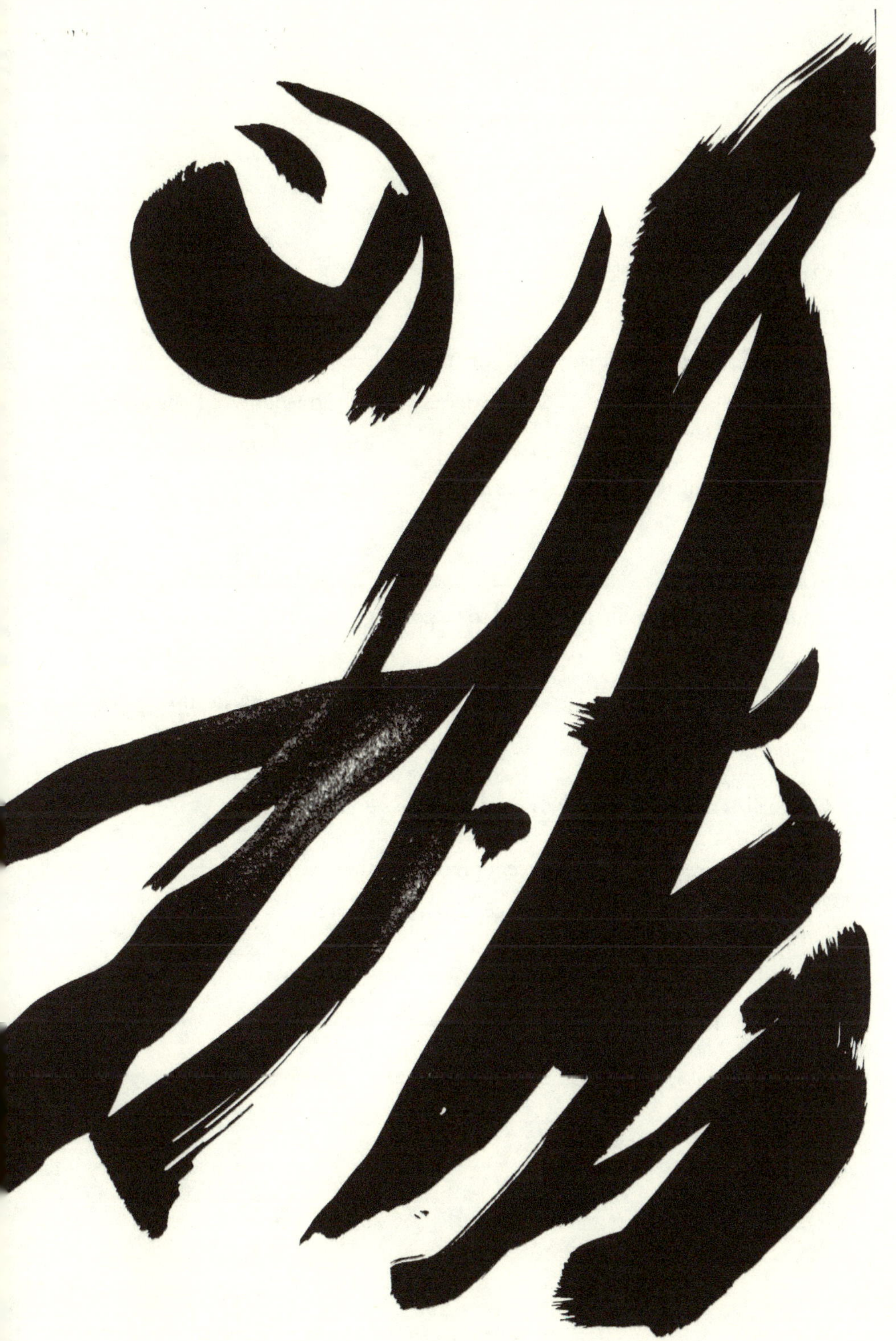

# Bangkok [neon lights]

O the orchids of Bangkok!

O the luxuriant ladyboys    their devilish seductive smiles
O the decadence    the freedoms of Bangkok!
your serpentine ways
into another unawares our embrace defined night-days

one thinks in embraces
young girls from the village pretend to be go-go girls

naked from waist up

city girls completely naked
Go-go girls dancing like embarrassed sardines

in the lady-boy club    an effervescent pretend land    Miss Brazil
Miss Mexico    Miss France    Miss Singapore
surgically amplified

in another bar

birds breathless up cunts

ping pong balls inserted   being thrown out

birds flying out of cunts

needles & needles being pulled out out of cunts

a whole string of sharp needles

razors being pulled out   a whole string

of razors being pulled out

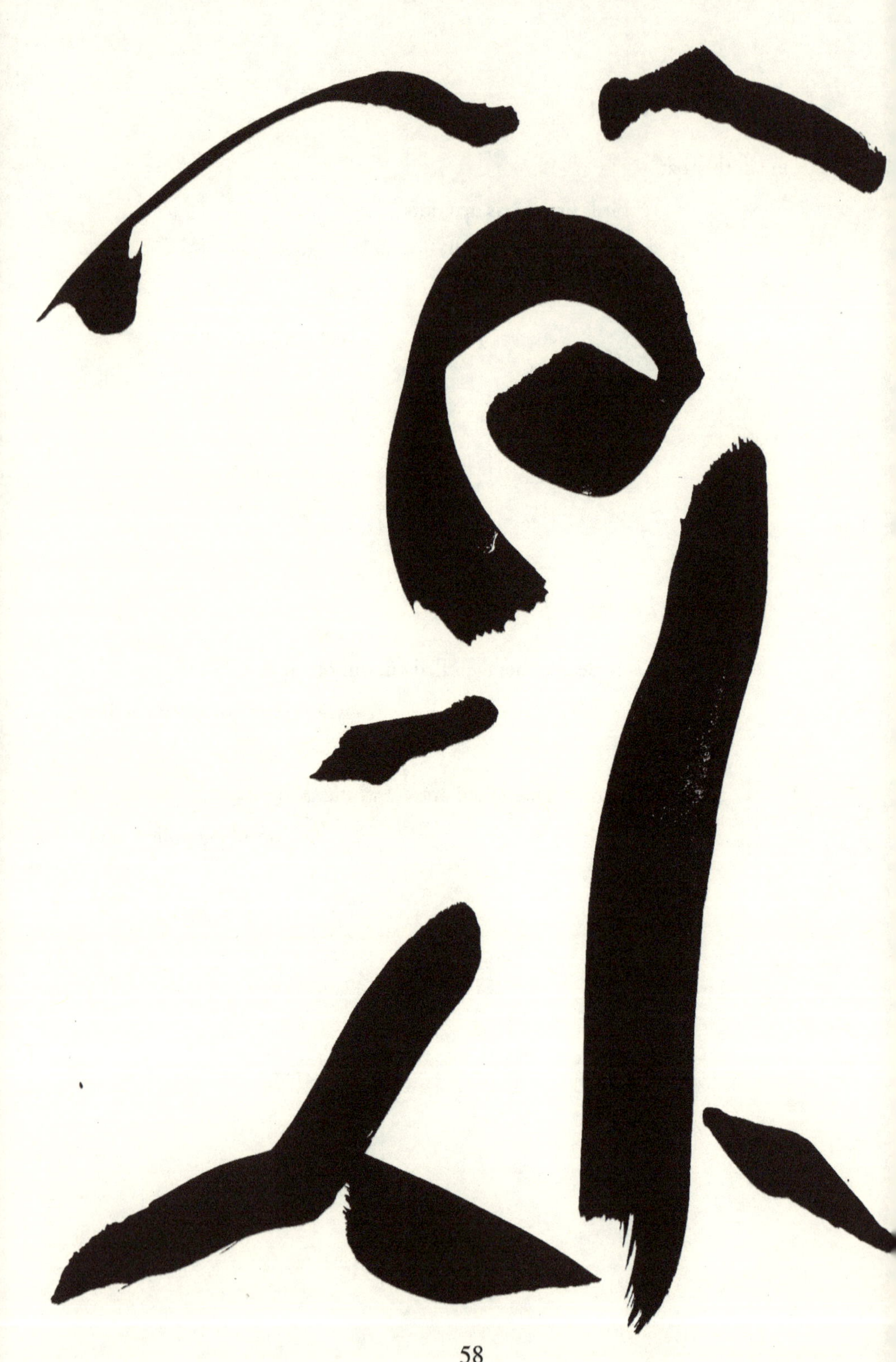

## Sentient Figure

*Wood Sculpture, Standing figure, 10th century. Indonesia.*

Ironwood man   boogie man
standing hands behind your ears   mouth gaping

Listen man!
hear the ants
you know them intimately
tribal enemies skinning heads on
the other coast
Knower   Listener
to what do you listen
what do you hear?

how are we destroying   ourselves
tell me this
the world's forests recede into a baldness

waves recede with great
momentum

there is no way into the other world but by listening   watching

nothing to do but

BREATHE

Breathe   listen to the forest leaves rustling

breathe   listen to the iron lungs of the world

wooden lungs of the forests

red muscular lungs of roots

beating hearts of skittish cats

loyal hearts of buffalos wading

the whoosh of unrelenting waves

families have gone   evacuated

fierce winds   blow   howling man

Quiet Man!

a great man-eating wave has come!

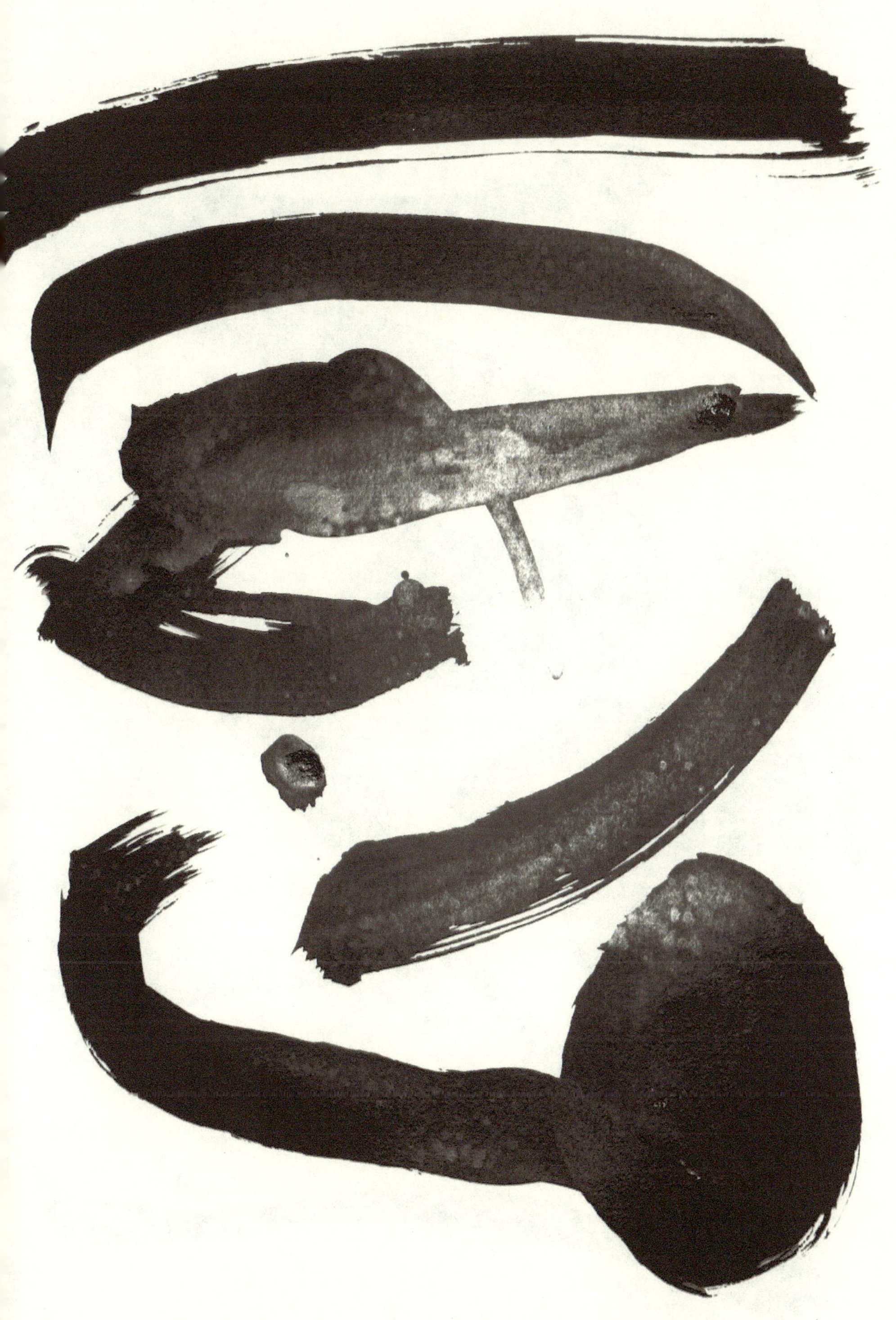

*Mộng Lan, Tokyo, July 2006*

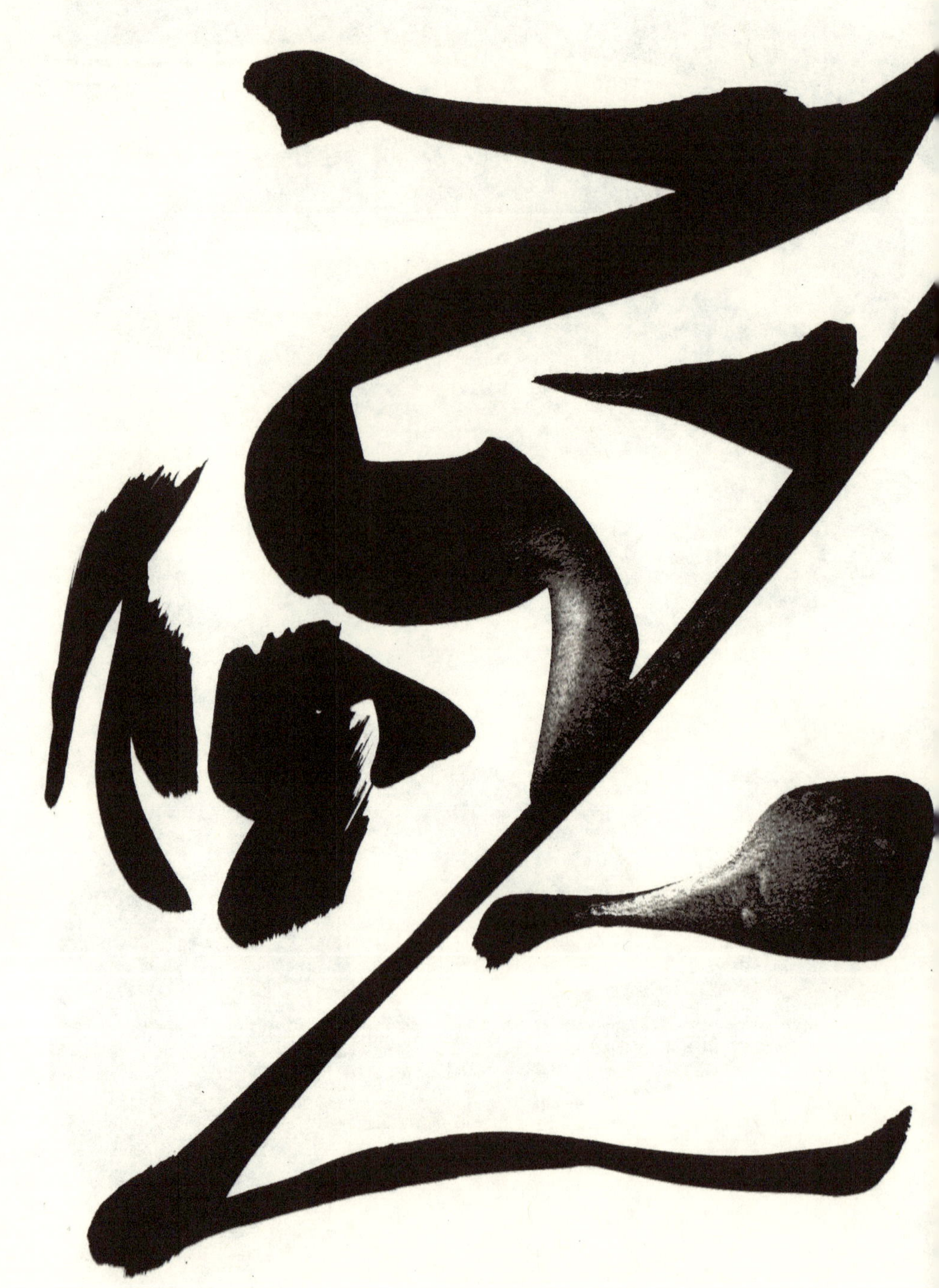

# Navigation

Tell    the coincidences
                    by which we navigate

                              where the incisions
                                        by which were wounds?

the symptoms may be alleviated    but the source still ails

                                          body is mind's servant

# Hallucination with Clay

# Desert Mysticism

1

a woman wanders fur-
ther into the mountains
rock so smooth you would sacrifice your life
to touch it

sweaty green hardness
insatiate cactus
festers
this water reflects the bathers' voices
back sides of a cool animal
birch trees texture of skin

through danger  related

she descends

2

laughter echoing bathers
water swells of melted snow
pools of antennas green-blue algae
she has gone fur-
ther into the
depths

smooth stone underside of a cool animal
above jagged lines
belly to stone the bathers lie sprawled a city

chasm side of black green

streams tread cracks  white twine

echoes of what was here
yesterday    now
hallucinogenic hands

& feet      voice (flesh)  shot onto rock
a mirror boasting
erosion  waterfalls molecules slip through black

3

chiseled earth's face

the sun chases

the torpid mountains

abruptly a skein

of moon

## 4

between skin & blood

between barkskin & stream    lull in water & air
                                        (lull of what *was* water    now air)
            climbing  aware of everything

there is no destiny involved in this take out destiny

                                        birds  burst      for lack

5

silence's surf   frayed edge
follows the path winding

the scraggy sides  trails irrepressible
a needle green fusion
take hundreds of years to form taking
the form to realize

the eye to see

let world slide

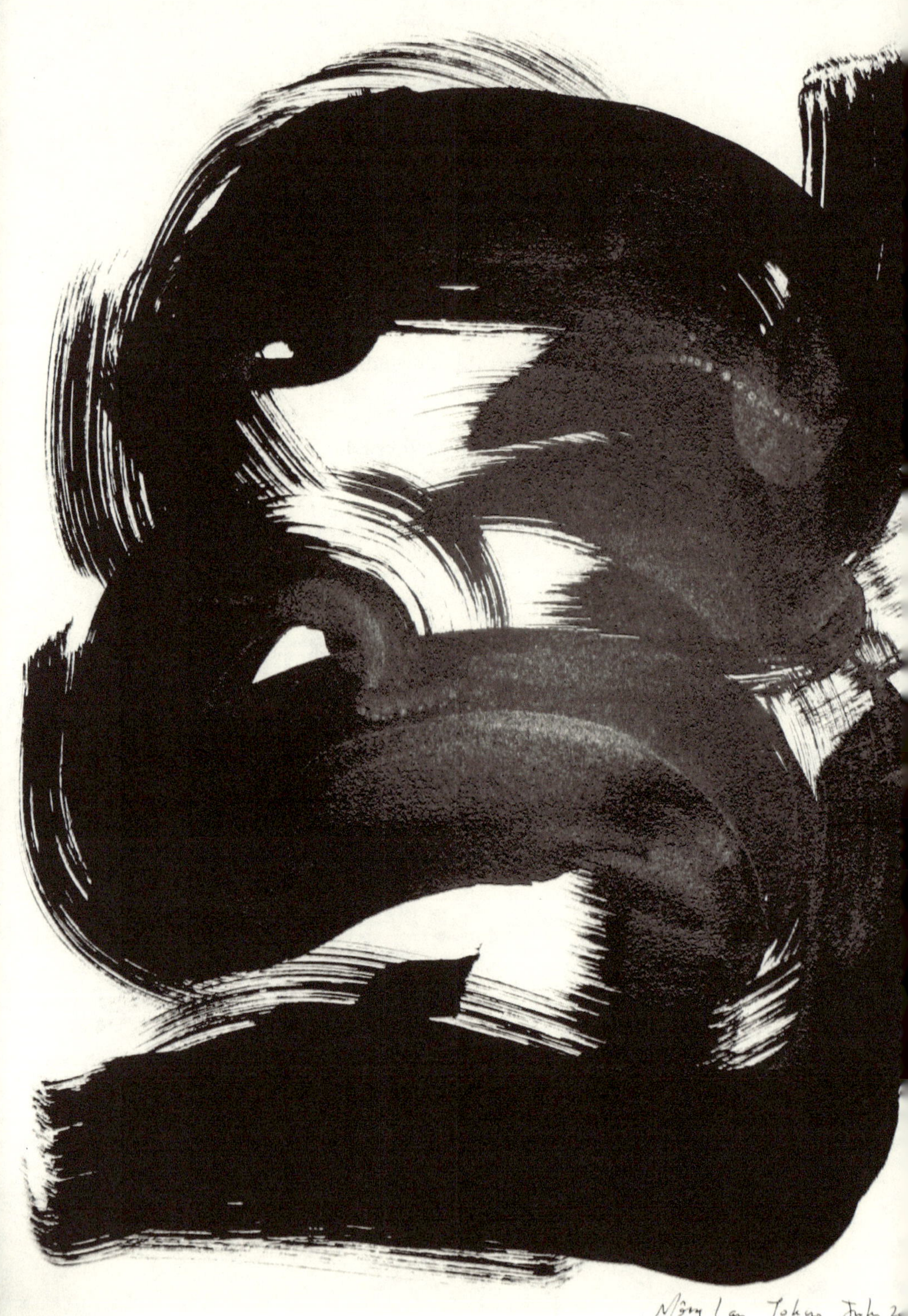
Mộng Lan, Tokyo, July

6

sky falls nonchalant luster

i am dying

in your thought

(sit still   wind)

i cut the tendons

of darkness   music & stars

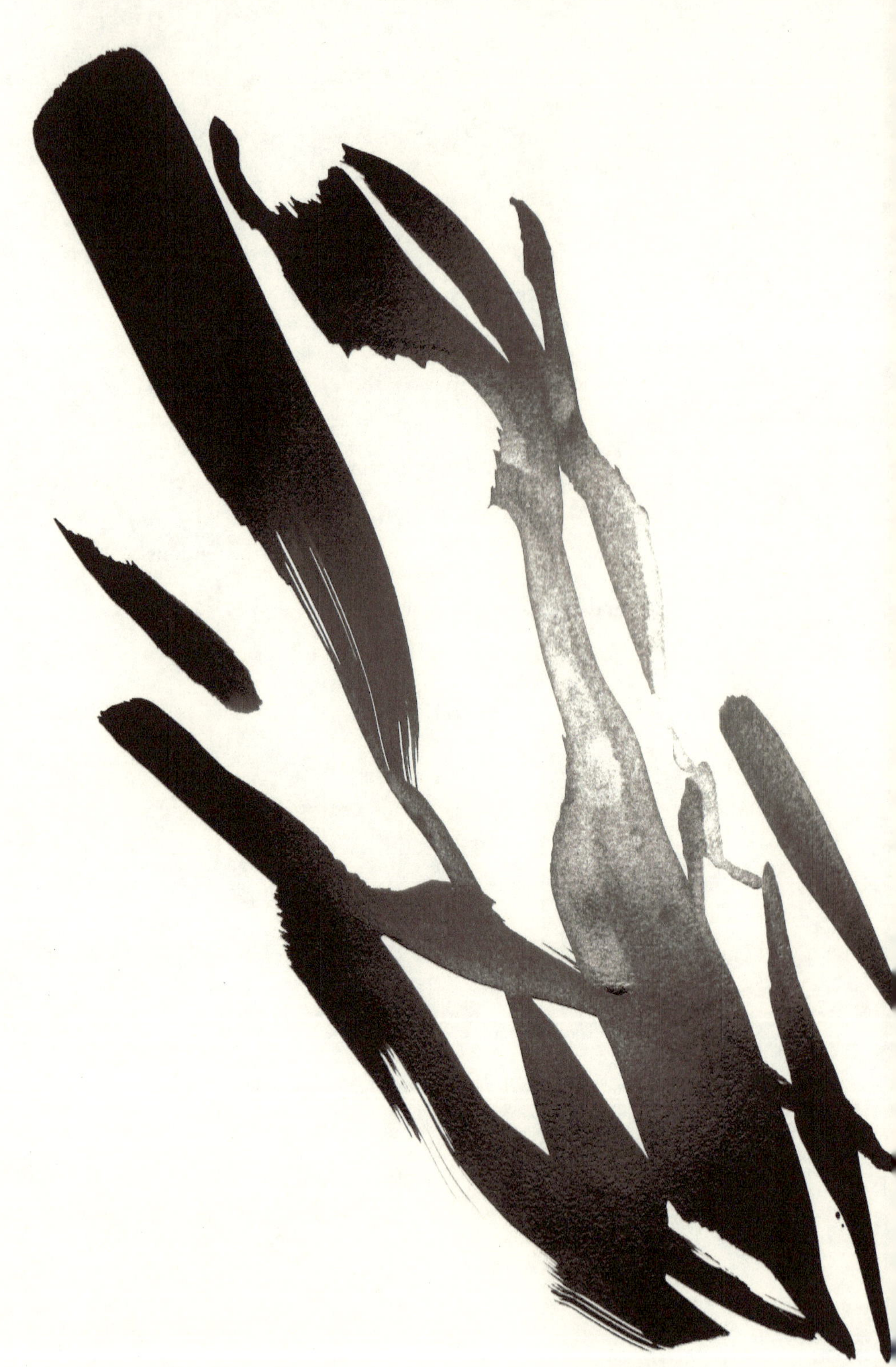

## Mountain Mysticism

1

Shuffling suede footprints
snarled coyote's tongues

mountain's clustered knuckles
blanket a land of haikus
rubber shoes leave trails of thoughts   fishhook of
dust blown   questing

a lady notes the spectacular view
slashed granite  & lichen curdling

the "phoneline trail"
grinds muscles
down moving slopes upwardly sloping

desert flowers red velvet against dirt
a yellow breeze fosters green lichen

death pervasive as sweat
over the saguaro's proud & lusty stubble
burnt out thick saguaro man with ambiguous arms

2

you have scaled to the top    rocks carved by rain

range by heat  &  plodding feet of strangers

so many have trod here  over rim stubble created by

exhaustion          &          avalanches

wind warp tethers dirt in eyes

scares ghostly feet

words crusted from lips straggling on dust paths

ancient eyes carved this path through the Sabino canyons  albino & wise

a rock kicked out of place          pocketed as souvenir

3

stone

is matter haunted with sounds

voice-eating

shuffling eyes    howling

like coyotes

4

if we are not all travelers      what are we?

                    if we are not ultimately ephemeral      what are we?

if not travelers from another world      which world?

                              we are permanence itself

                                    why dare we self-destruct?

[Tucson, Arizona, 2000]

# Desert: What is Left

## 1

*The Sonoran desert, Tucson, Arizona.*

thunder strikes the saguaro's arms orange
flares shoot
a dusky symphony

the desert   a stalwart sandy shore
without sea or port

at night  i walk under the sea

adoring arms of cacti          gouging darkness
underwater vegetation     bending  curious          alive   at home

a rattlesnake sky curls over  nervy mountains

the saguaro dreams of water
wasps eat the stars

## 2

night divulges a starry map on earth's roof

i walk at night to the mountains
climbing the mauve land                    near rattlesnakes

the sky curls its fingers
under an earth's iridescent skirt

lack of water one hallucinates with the reserved clay
loquacious skies   howling stillness of the desert
cacti live on a drop of water a year
yet live for hundreds of years

here   a dead rabbit   a dead goat
a dead cat                    a dead woman

sleeping in the leaves of the *palo verde*

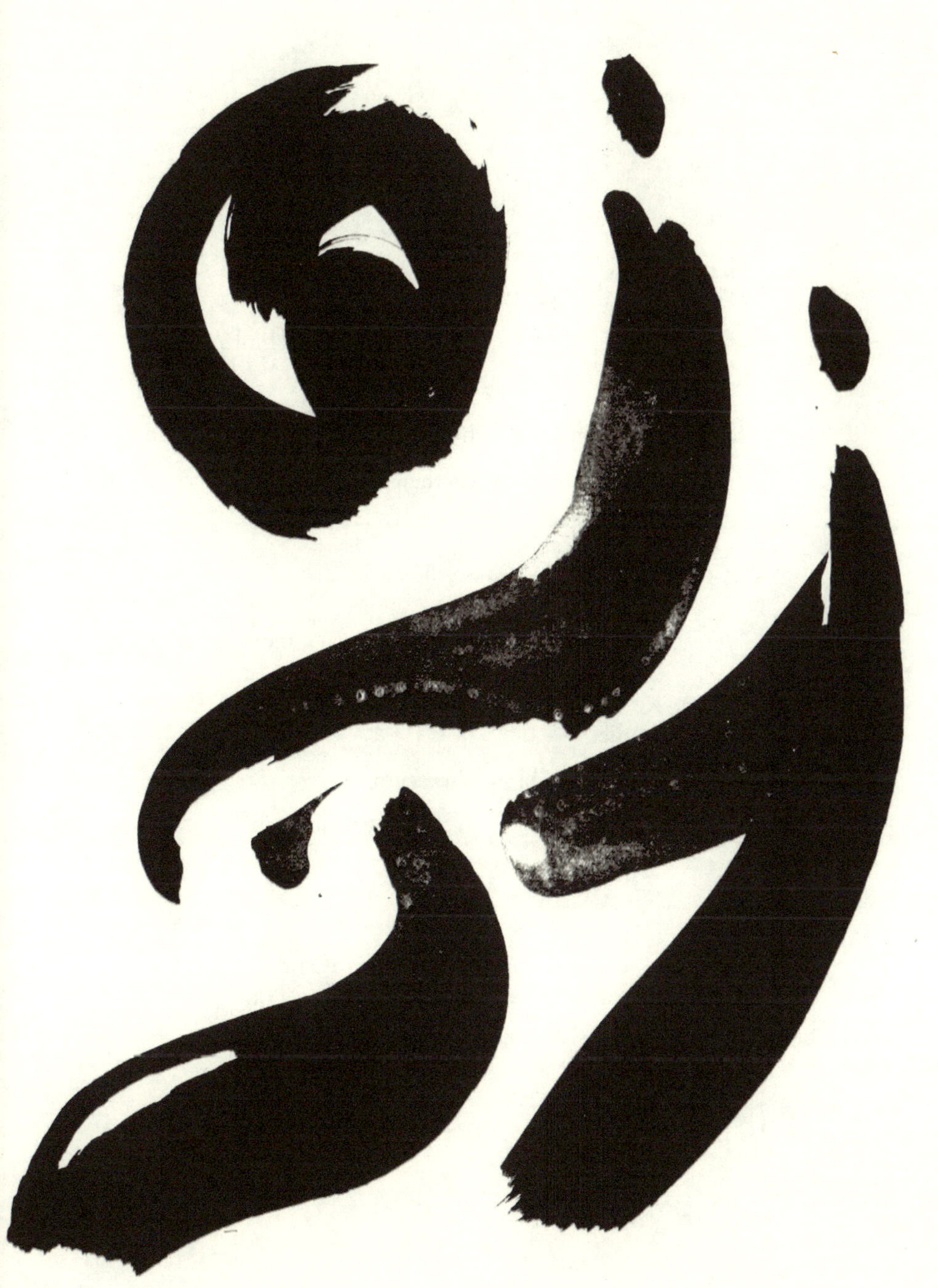

# The Bodywasher

Najaf, Iraq

i read the violence on their charred flesh
embattled limbs

sand black shards & itchy wind 120 F heat are etched
on their skins

they turn up with help i wash them

morning to night
rain-like they appear
suicide bombers' bodies
of blood dirt scum
& wild
desires

young boys soldiers after the calling
of Jihad

§

i turn them over their clay skin
like sleeping fish
wash them clean & pure
until the sins washed away the body
reflecting unnatural light

my father was a body washer so was my mother
& my father's father
i hope my son will *not* follow me

it's tiring to know
so much about someone's
dead body
assuaging their spiritless bones

their souls flown to Allah the virgins
waiting

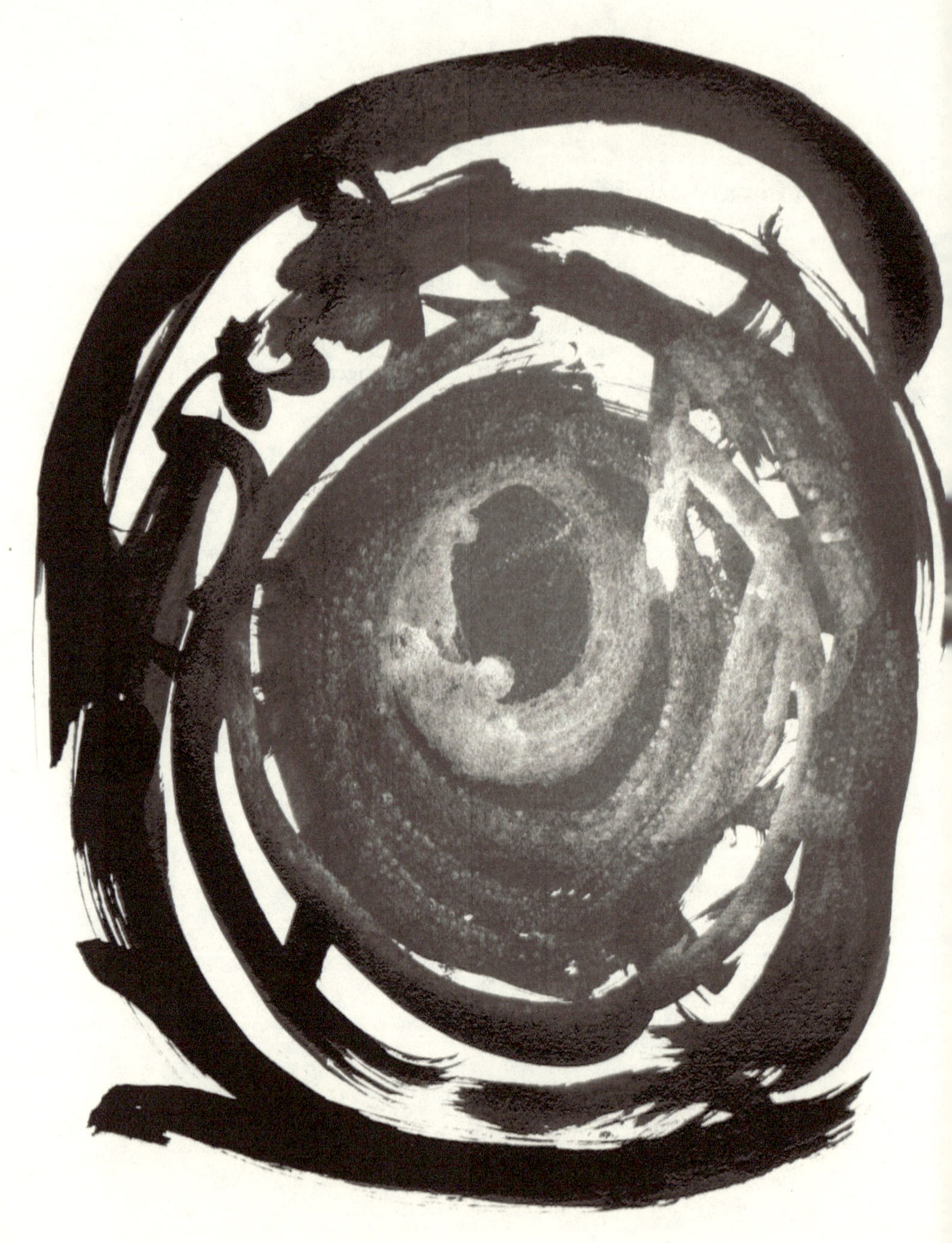

§

a suicide bomber blows up in a mosque

a suicide bomber crosses into Palestine

a suicide bomber crosses into Israel

a suicide bomber disappears into a bar in Bali

a suicide bomber waits to be called upon

# Flight

1

large metallic grey pigeons
warm benign
creatures
with gentle curves
landing  taking off

other times  like sharks
B-52 planes  a friend of a friend
flew them in Iraq

the hospital planes like slim messengers
from the heavens to
administer the sick
are all on duty now

2

what a thrill to see planes
land take off there is a simple physics
to the matter an irrefutable beauty

two large wings a tail a head
of metal steel yet adroitly
curved from a distance
thunderous from above

steel flying into the heavens

at Yokota Airbase flight
is of essence
a plane an advancement
of nature

3

at night the take-off-landing lights blare green red
Christmas lights
any of these planes could be flying
off to the Middle East Afghanistan Iraq
Korea Katmandu
Germany Indonesia or Italy

the planes serve mightily
serve well
they swerve
to the east west
north & south

tame following
their pilot's wishes their metal noses
serve only to direct not smell

a plane is lifted into the air
by the propulsion underneath
& soars

## 4

O grey airplane

where have you been?

in which country were you on mission?—

[Yokota Airbase, Japan 2002-2005]

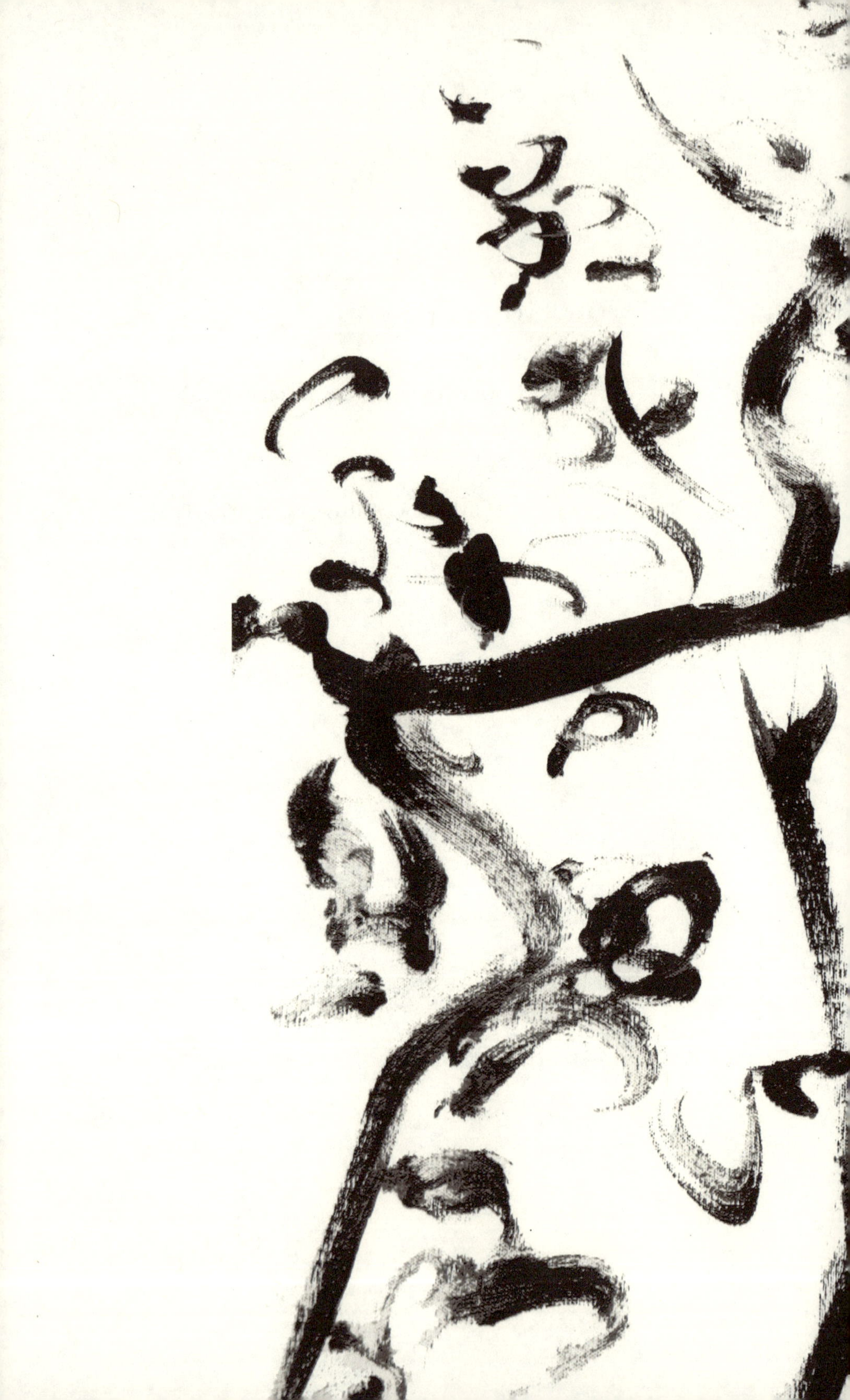

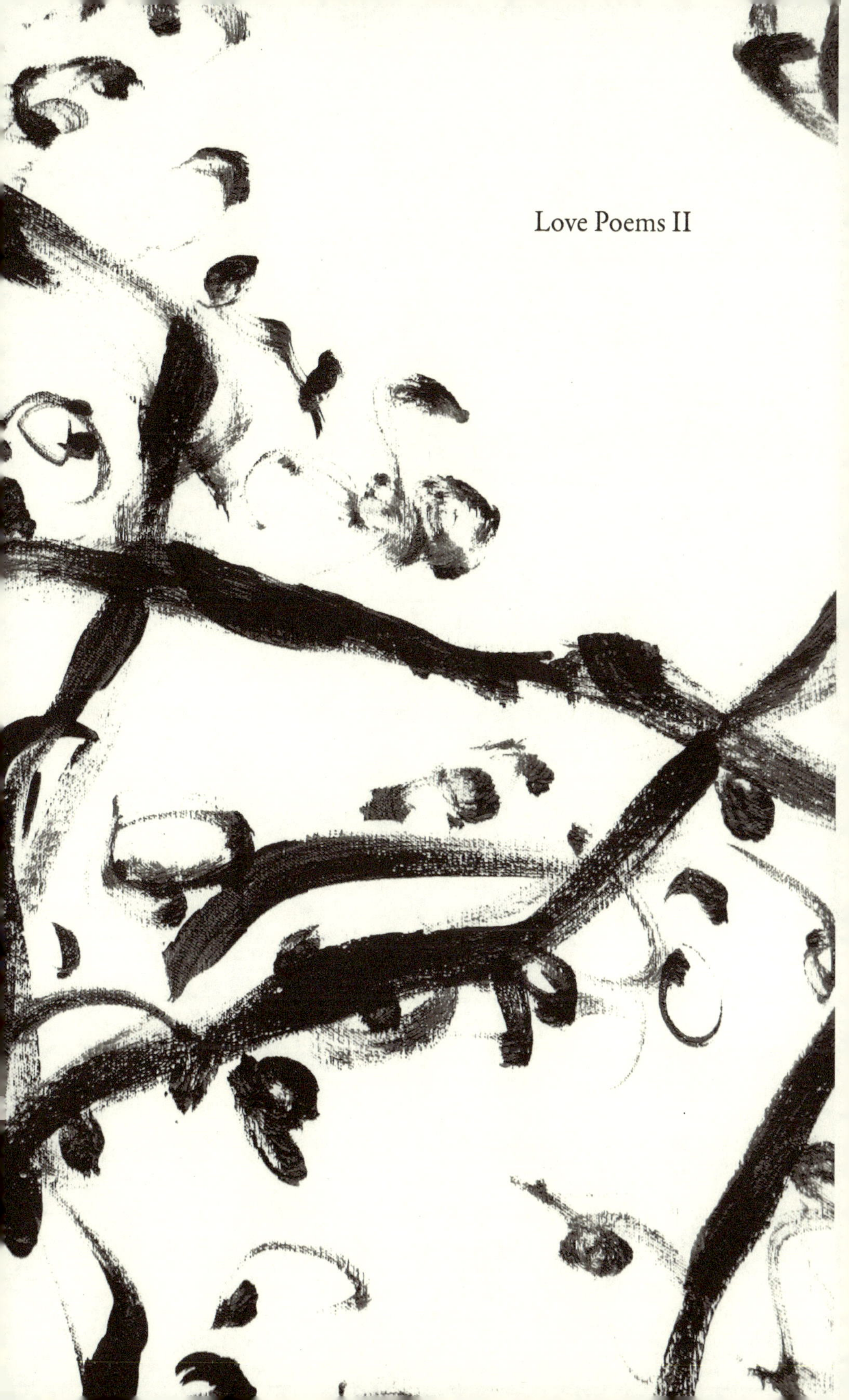

# Love Poems II

## Love Poem to *Café au Lait*

you wake me up every morning
with your creaminess & smooth
talking body    brown
& supple    muscles
dexterous    inviting

your caramel & froth
sing to me in French
and i sing in French all day Edith Piaf
her sparrowlike songs
with a bit of sugar    it is amazing
how you bring me to an addictive frenzy

white frizzy fuzz    your brown-white
moustache    your milky otherness
your stunning inkiness
that would write odes    ballads    and novels
that would build railroads
& skyscrapers    fences & automobiles    skyrockets

Civilization itself

you are nothing like the *café sữa*

of my Sài Gòn which is exceedingly sweet

bitter & concentrated like Sài Gòn itself

O *Café au Lait* i know you hum

sweet nothings and ideas

into other's ears

i only wait for you to drive

me crazy inflict an ulcer

perhaps I should give you up

for something more gentle faithful

like green tea?

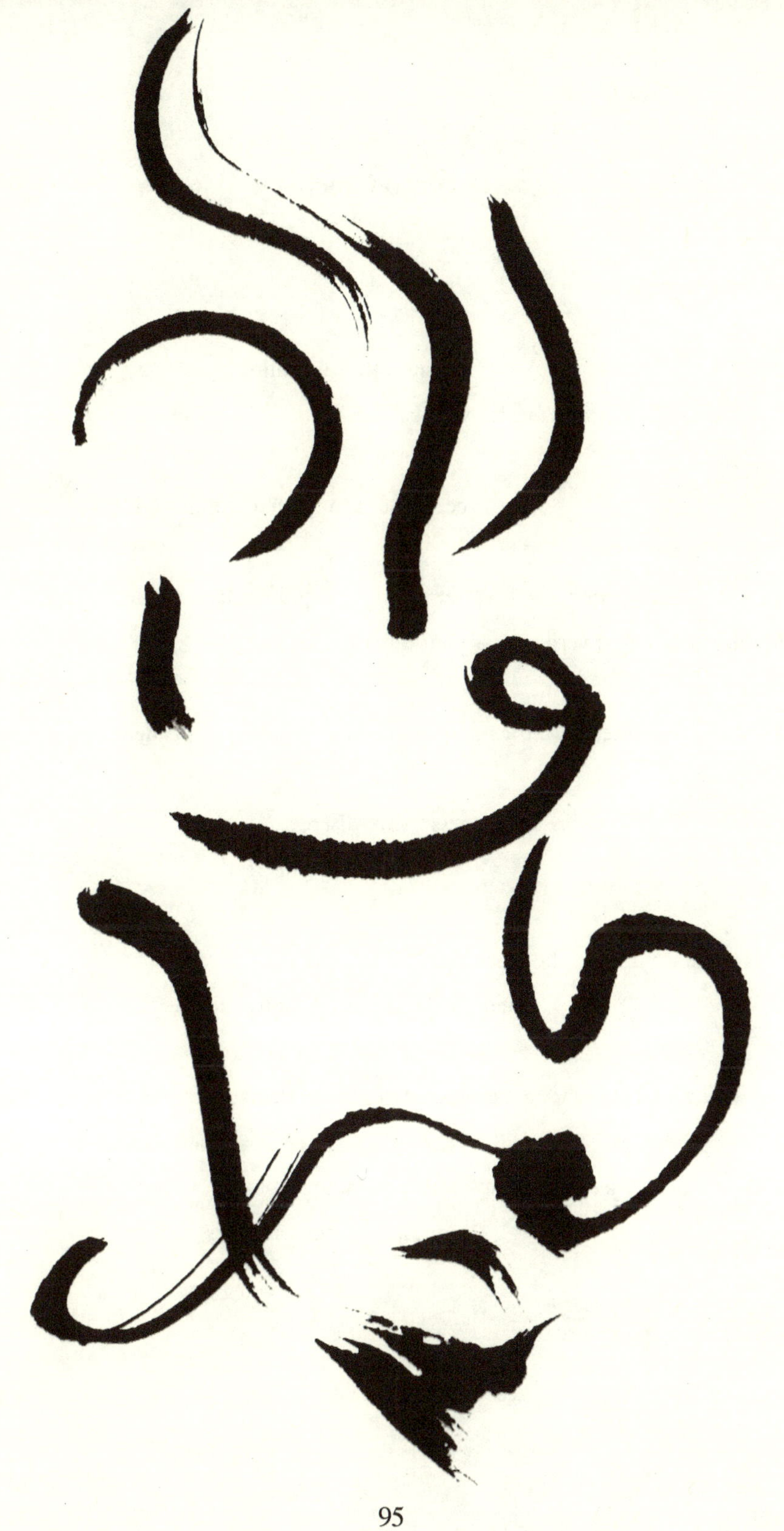

## Love Poem to Green Tea

smooth    unassuming   low-key
i have left *café au lait* for you darling

left the coffee bean for your   complicated
yet pure leaf
your body          emerald   tranquil    a slant rhyme
underneath this clear verdigris   is your inner self

underneath the unassuming demeanor is your prudent

uniqueness    your discreet
fluid whispers

you give me strength in the mornings
when the day is low    you give me energy

your powers so steady they are enacted without the drinker's knowing

sleek   lustrous   sage     sending me waves of bright
undulating   consciousness

## Love Poem to Garlic

stinking rose
the heady scent of you
tangy spicy
most underrated
year-round orb
bulbous root     incandescent moon

invoked as deities by the Egyptians     garlic
each day with you is another day tripled

stripped of your delicate covers your
fire-spitting fresh
rawness

i love you   unadulterated
a shiver once i bite you

medicinally you are a miracle
fighting colds          blood thinner
anti-bacterial extraordinaire

how to eat you raw    & love it:
peel the placenta-like cover
julienne
into fish sauce with red chili peppers lemon

your bold paleness exposed
i imagine you
at every moment

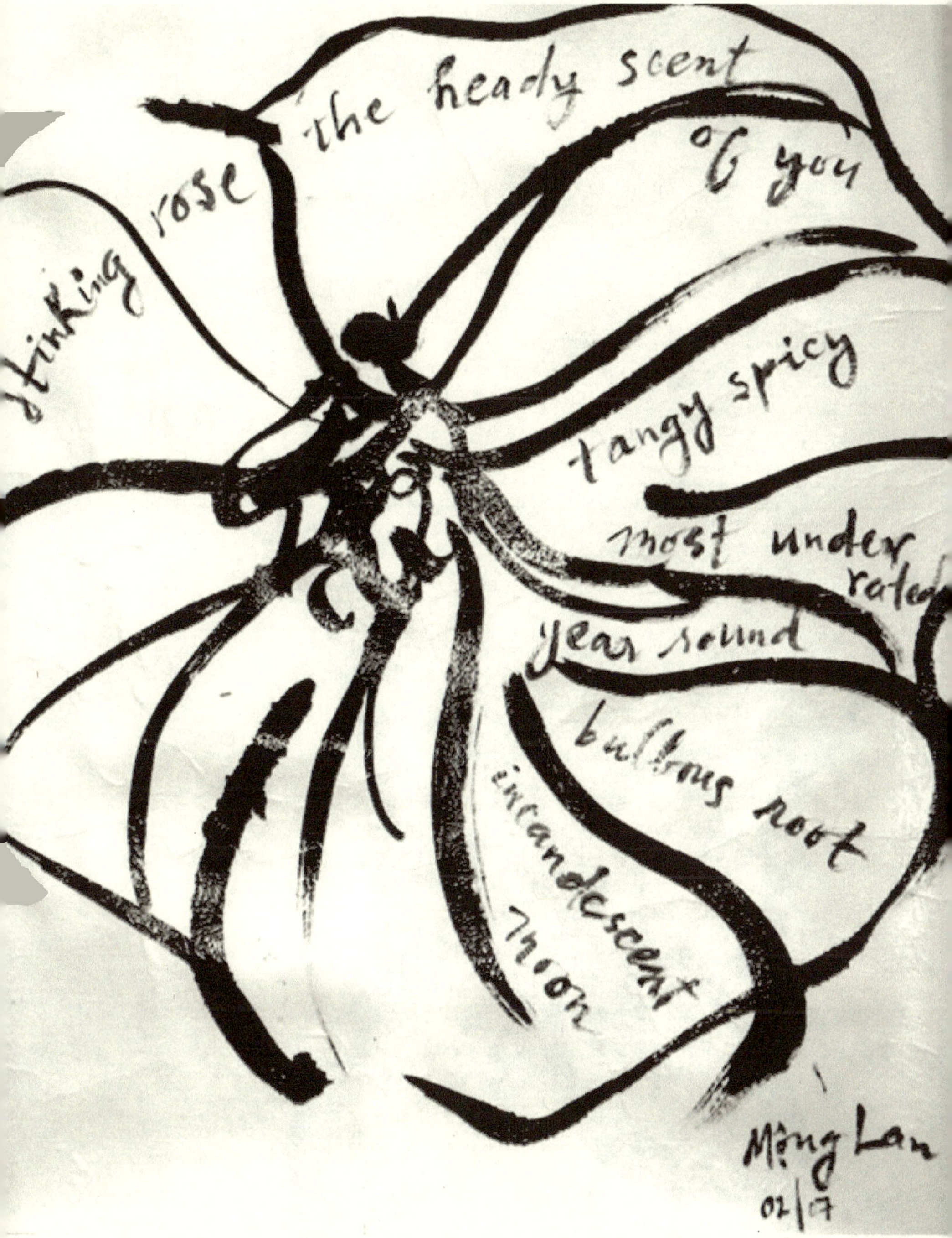

stinking rose the heady scent
of you

tangy spicy

most under
rated

year round

bulbous root

incandescent
moon

Mộng Lan
02/17

## Love Poem to Basil

in my garden  i

grow you

Asian basil  Italian basil

a sweet scent

emanates

lilting

a leaf

sings

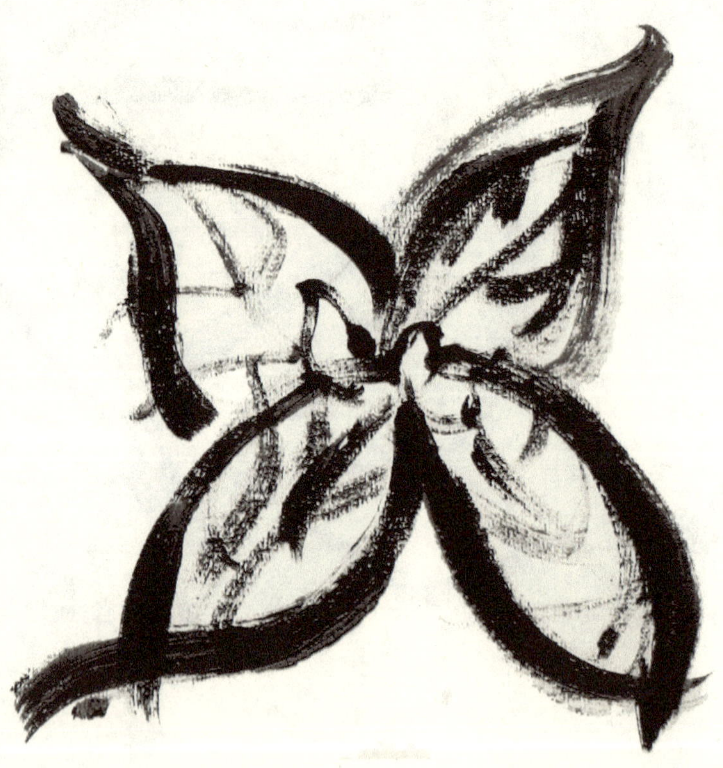

## Love Poem to Onion

the layers of you   how can i uncover?

*Allium cepa* of the amaryllis family
succulent pungent bulb

peeling by hand
the layers of your skin
layers needed to delve into you

skirts your physical body
of your past
your soul

cut raw
to get to the very core of you
i dive into you
rivers in place
how to plummet  how to sound out   the inner core?
you were powerful payment for builders
of the pyramids

as a child i planted you

watched your effervescent flowers

blow in the wind

then pulled you by the stalks

erudite onion  polyglot speaker
of many cultures

marinated in vinegar  cut into triangles

in my grief i eat you whole

purple yellow white

multitudinous colors of you

your many curvaceous smiles

bold orb  a moon white as my whitest sheet

your heart spotless

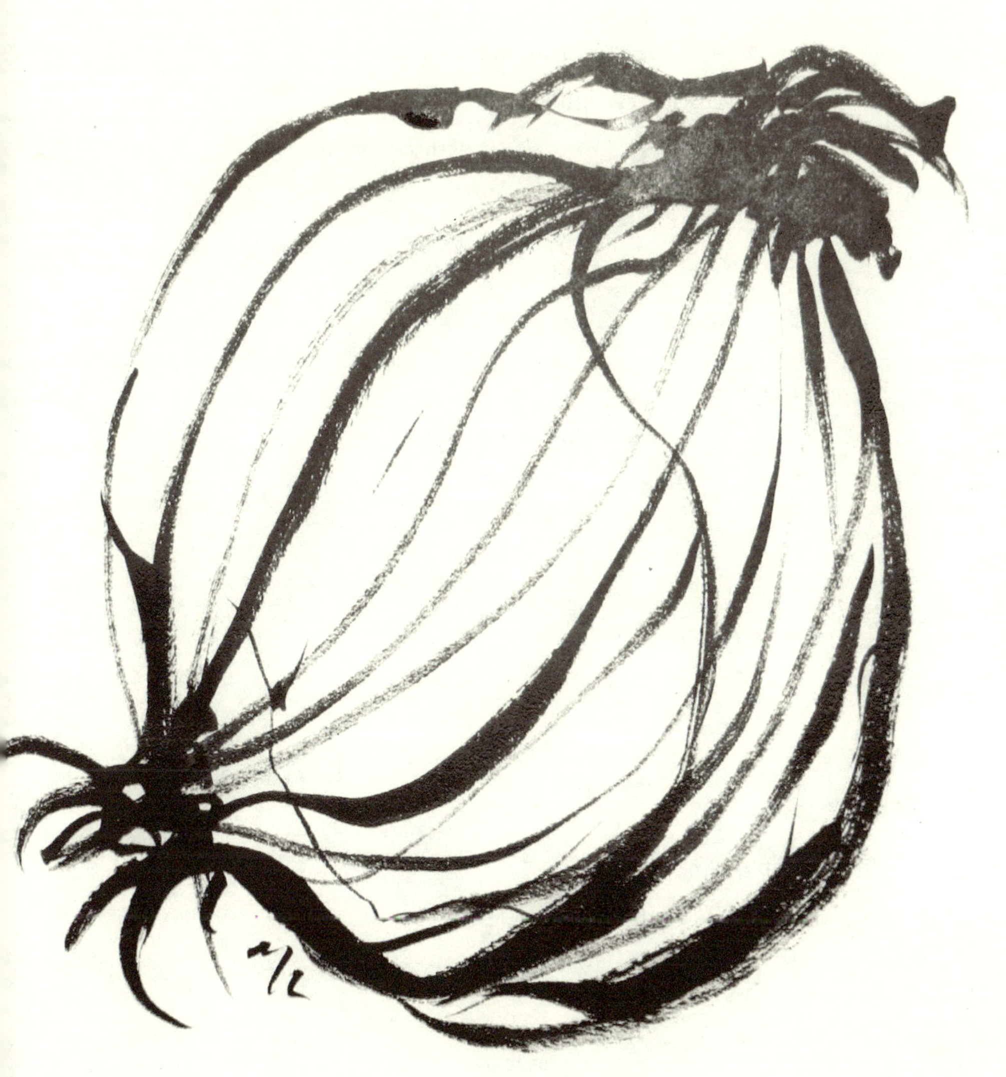

## Love Poem to Ginger

allayer of pain
*zingiber officinale*
strange root beige earth-lined
with sage wrinkles
wrangled
not with desire but to diffuse
desire

letting go—
this is how i let go of you
this is how
i let go

chop into small pieces
pour into water simmer
until the juices come out
how i let go

swirling tremor
drink until your heart desires
soother
of despair
slayer
O spicy rhizome!

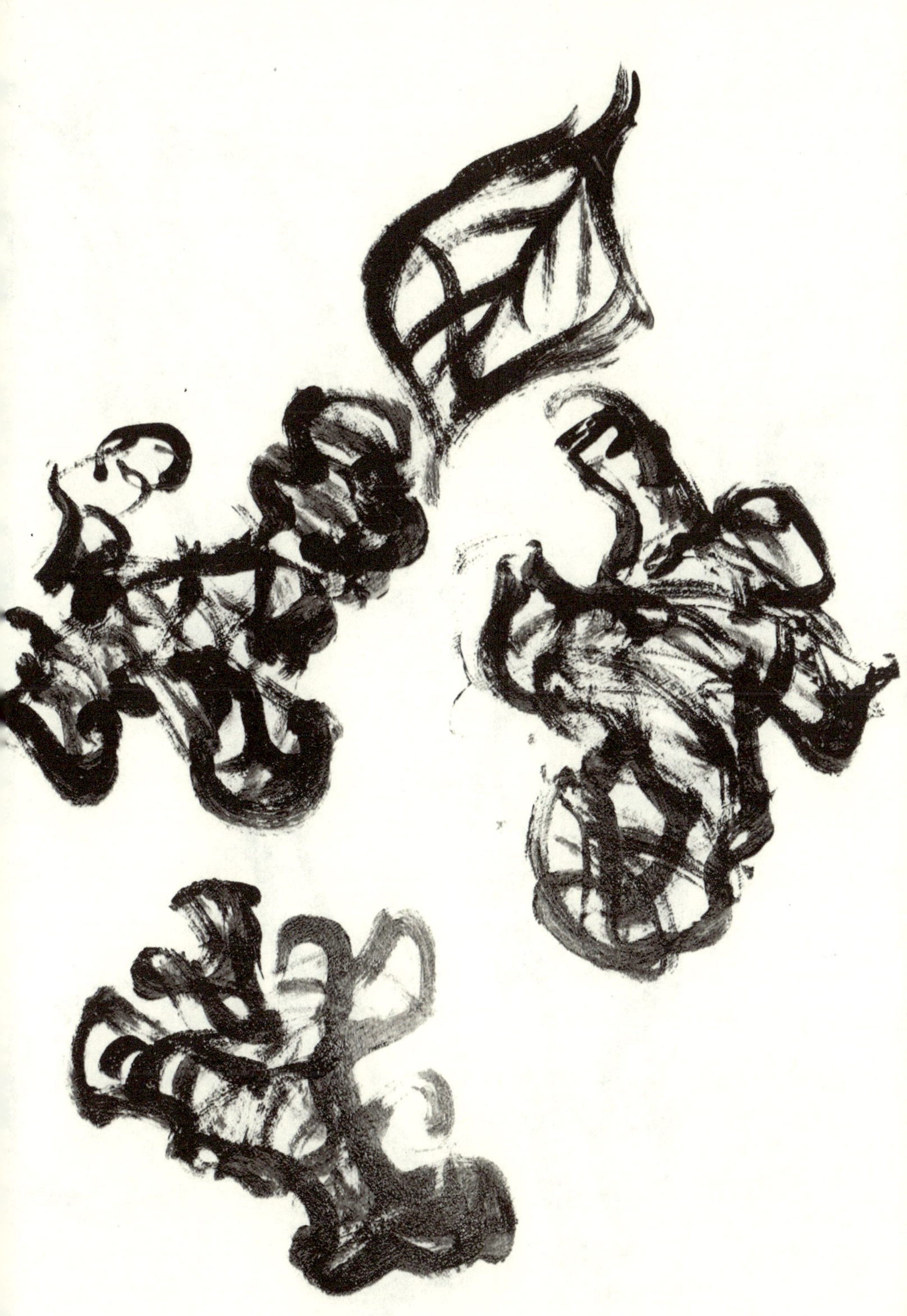

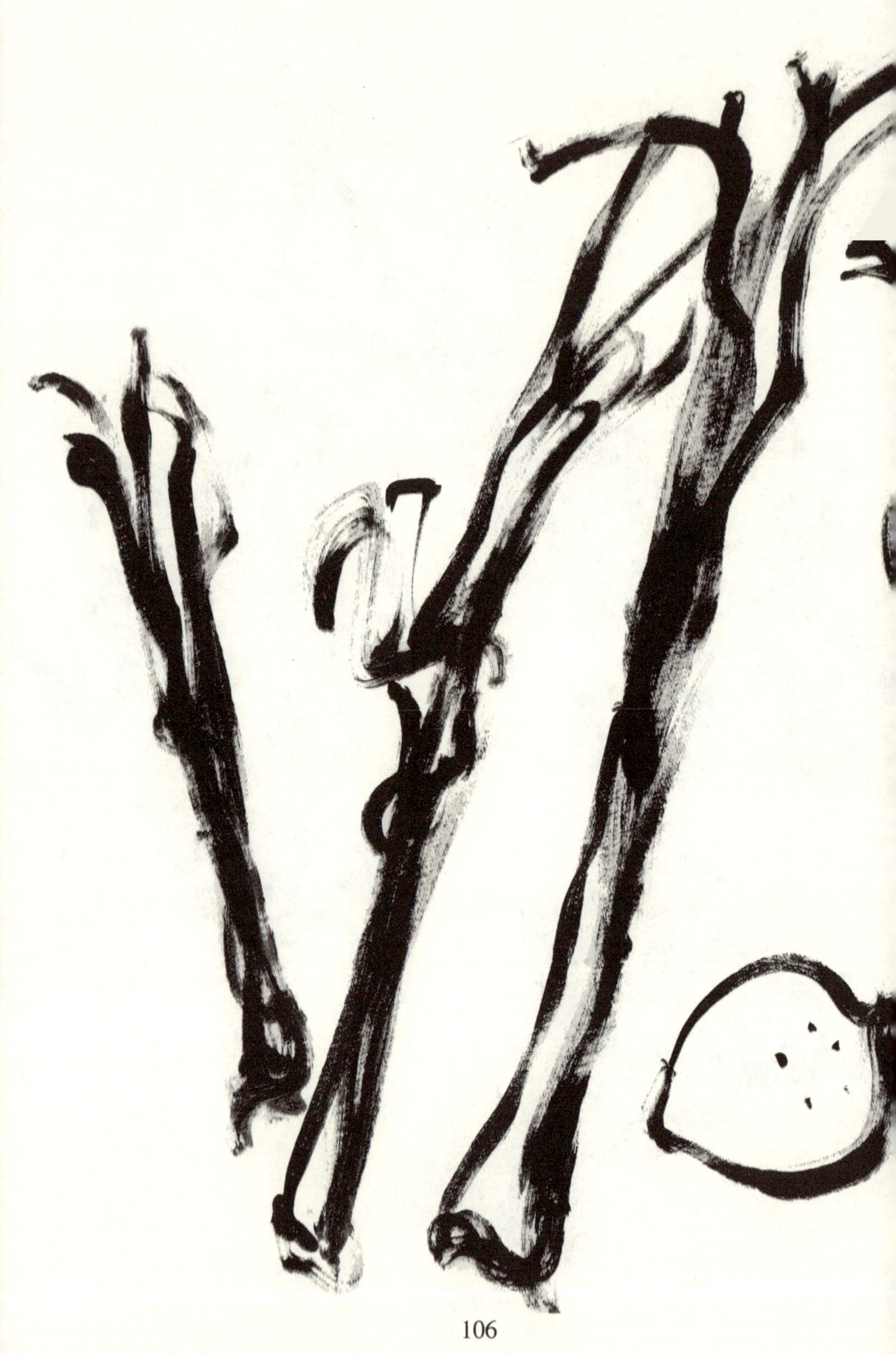

## Love Poem to Leeks

plain sautéed with garlic  in soups  stir fries
whatever the mood  whatever the season
i fold you  in

sheaf of green  sail of verdant thoughts
breezes  your warrior-like skin
i play on
your salient stalks
vital song of the earth
iron-rich  lovely your verdant form

sturdy  accountable  you beam greenly from the ground

tall leaves  O sheer ebullience
swarthy deepness  verity itself

fit sword

## Love Poem to Lemons

of my desserts filling my dreams
speaking to me in several languages

of my afternoons
of my nights
into my glass of water into olive oil
into soy sauce *nước mắm*
into the bitterest mildest blandest concoctions
i squeeze you into everything

a fervent
mirror
sourness brilliant as your color
your juice my lips pucker
your rinds i leave around to smell your vigor

bright burning desire
liquid yellow like creativity

your delivery is great
from a certain petiteness

dense yet your glowingness expansive

*as if* acidic

but actually alkaline

once in the body

famous detoxifier

delirious high C

trembling splash

squeaky thrill nonchalant

gold clear to the soul

## Love Poem to Soto

in Magelang  the first time i held
you   given to me by a kindly woman
who laughed when i said "no a*yam*" ("no chicken")
i expected nothing

you exist with such simplicity   broth
clear as a daffodil day
bean sprouts   tofu   tempe   cabbage   shallots
rice from the verdant paddies of Java

it's love at first taste

the first bowl of you quenches a physical hunger

the second quenches the hunger
in my soul

from each spoonful the mountains of Java unfolded Gunung Merapi
lush bananas  leaves beaconing
the jungles palm trees came forth
the terraced rice paddies unfolded
steppes of young strapling rice

with each spoonful   Borodudur unfolded each carved stone story
each Buddha each stupta
each memory of water and stone
yet to me
how familiar
you are   your sweet juices

by what routes did i come to you?
planes trains and buses

distances long and far away
how long have i dreamt of you distinct
as the *phở* of my Vietnam

the Javanese landscape glistens on your surface
your body swirling yellow with *kunyit* (tumeric)
a dawning sun
O *Soto* dancing
on my tongue
how long have i dreamt of you?

*For Komunitas Utan Kayu, with gratitude*

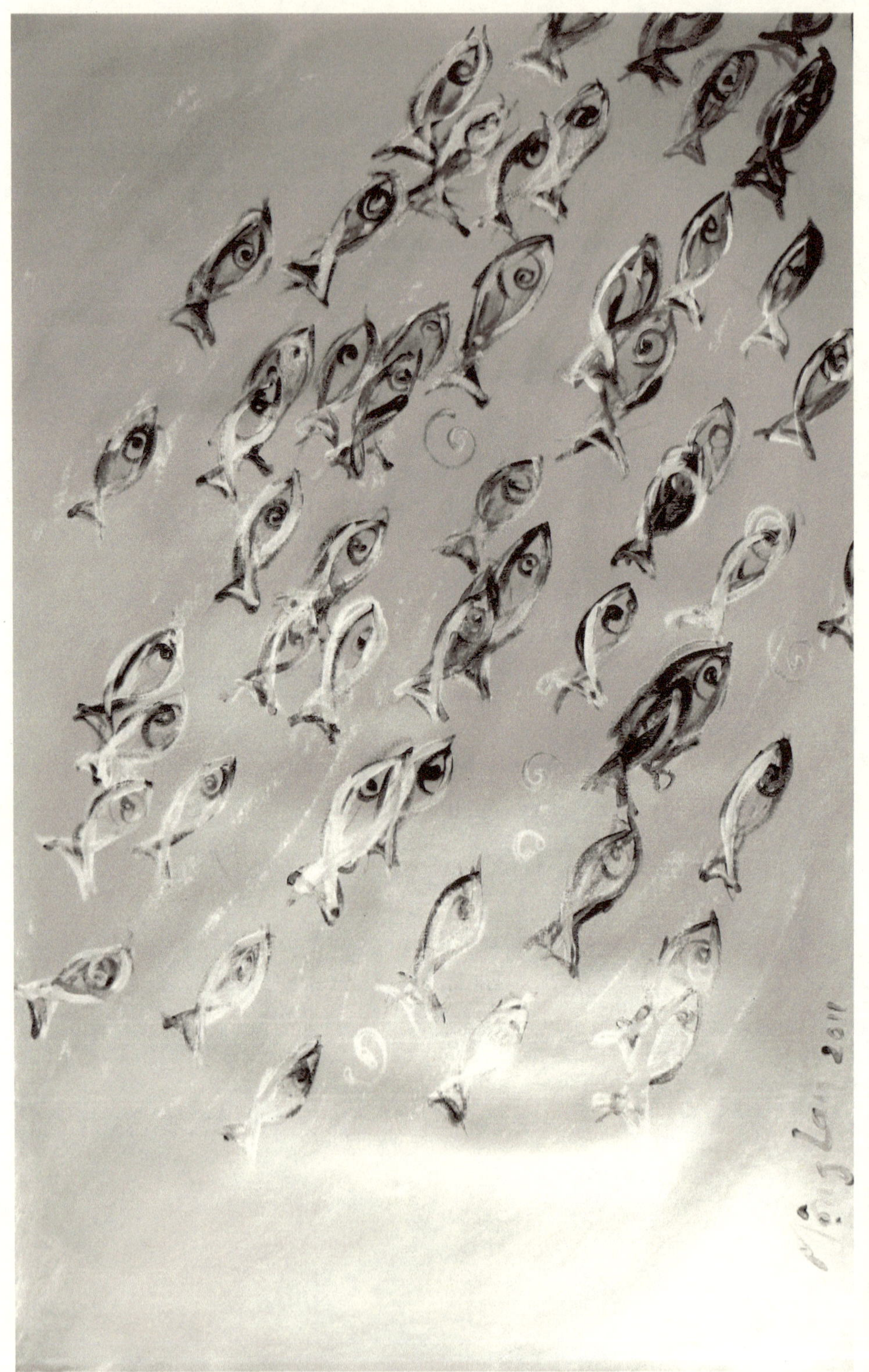

# Love Poem to *Nước Mắm*

O saucy
little fish    packed in vats    limed with salt
pressed
pressed until your bones are worn into the salt water
pressed until you no longer exist between the layers

until your essence of fish has been distilled    your protein extracted
until the essence of your soul  released

how long to distill you
from fish's bones
into a tangy sauce that is essential to the Vietnamese
and all of Southeast Asia?

from condiments  to rice dishes to noodles
your inner-most delights
spiked with chilies    lemons

how to let your inner soul fly?

wayward demon    watery inner angel
source of life

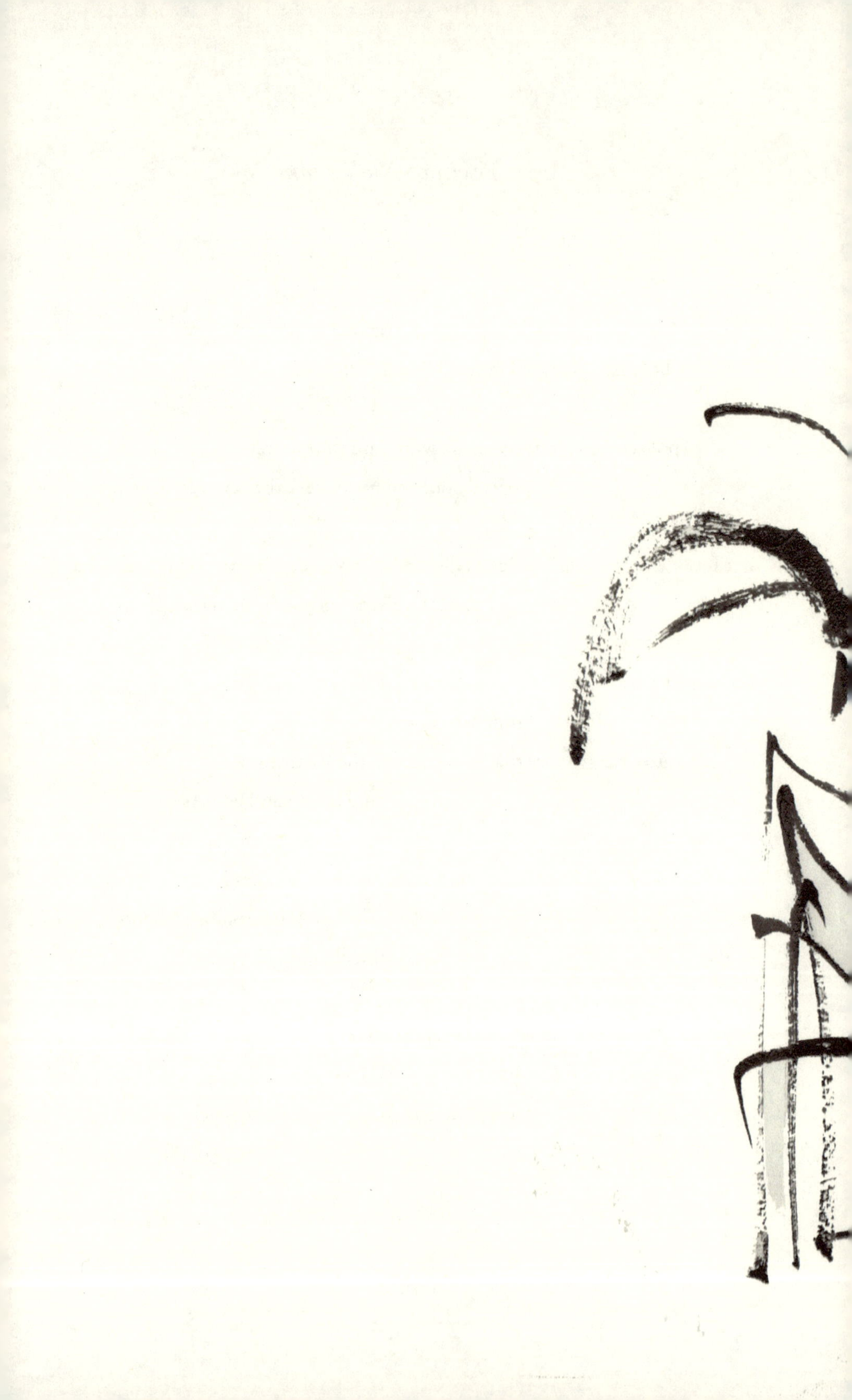

# Smoky Cities, Pigeons' Wings

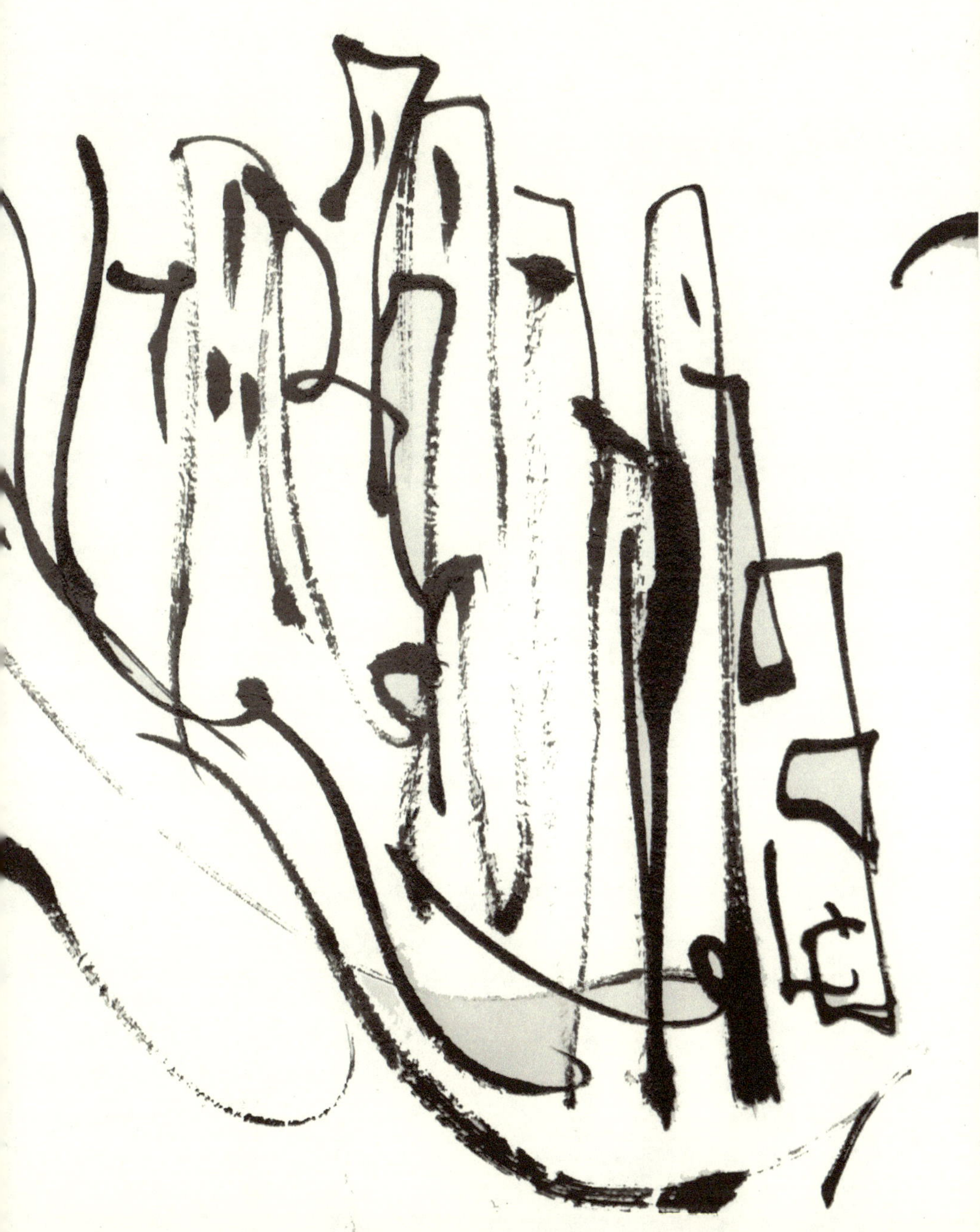

## Seoul Snow

smoky skeletons of trees

snow   ghostly        wet

Seoul awash in white snow over buildings cars roads
falling on the Han River

i wore a friend's mink coat  something i could never afford
nor want
(being alone
poetry starts from here)

city of bridges   extending into forever
of quick deals industrious hustling for emails
irons in the fire

thinking of Seoul's cold &

my friend's warmth  her lack of English  her expensive
apartment overlooking the river
the three cell phones she carries with her     the three
packs of cigarettes she smokes a day

smoke in cafés where women
with mink coats  go

smoke in her car  smoke before lunch   during
between servings & after lunch

she writes of actors  actresses    interviews them
they call her up
desiring interviews to make them
famous  bloated like snow

smoke in traffic   Seoul rush hour
bumper to bumper smoke

## Upon seeing Marcel Marceau in Buenos Aires

Speechless  he was & will always be
not for words as he does not need them

a motion of the finger  he lifts up the sun
chagrinned grin

under spotlight on the Teatro Grand Rex's stage in Buenos Aires
he mimes
as if on the humble streets of Paris

mining not  for a *franc*  but for Art
the hearts of those watching

one graceful gesture in complete silence
a complete paragraph
an old man becomes
splendidly young
nimble
spritely
splendor in the spot-
light

stuck in his bird

cage his own heart

hands flying like doves' wings leaving his body

a feminine motion of the hip the eye smiles

goes through the motions

of a life birth youth middle age old age

in the court case he is everybody

at once judge

prosecutor defense victim perpetrator

& gets hanged

flexibly humane

a grand master of mimicry

knowing too well the final fate of humanity

of 84 years of living

& thus the last world tour

nothing remembered

compares with

his deliberate hypnotic movements

a single light

a bird flies from his winged hands

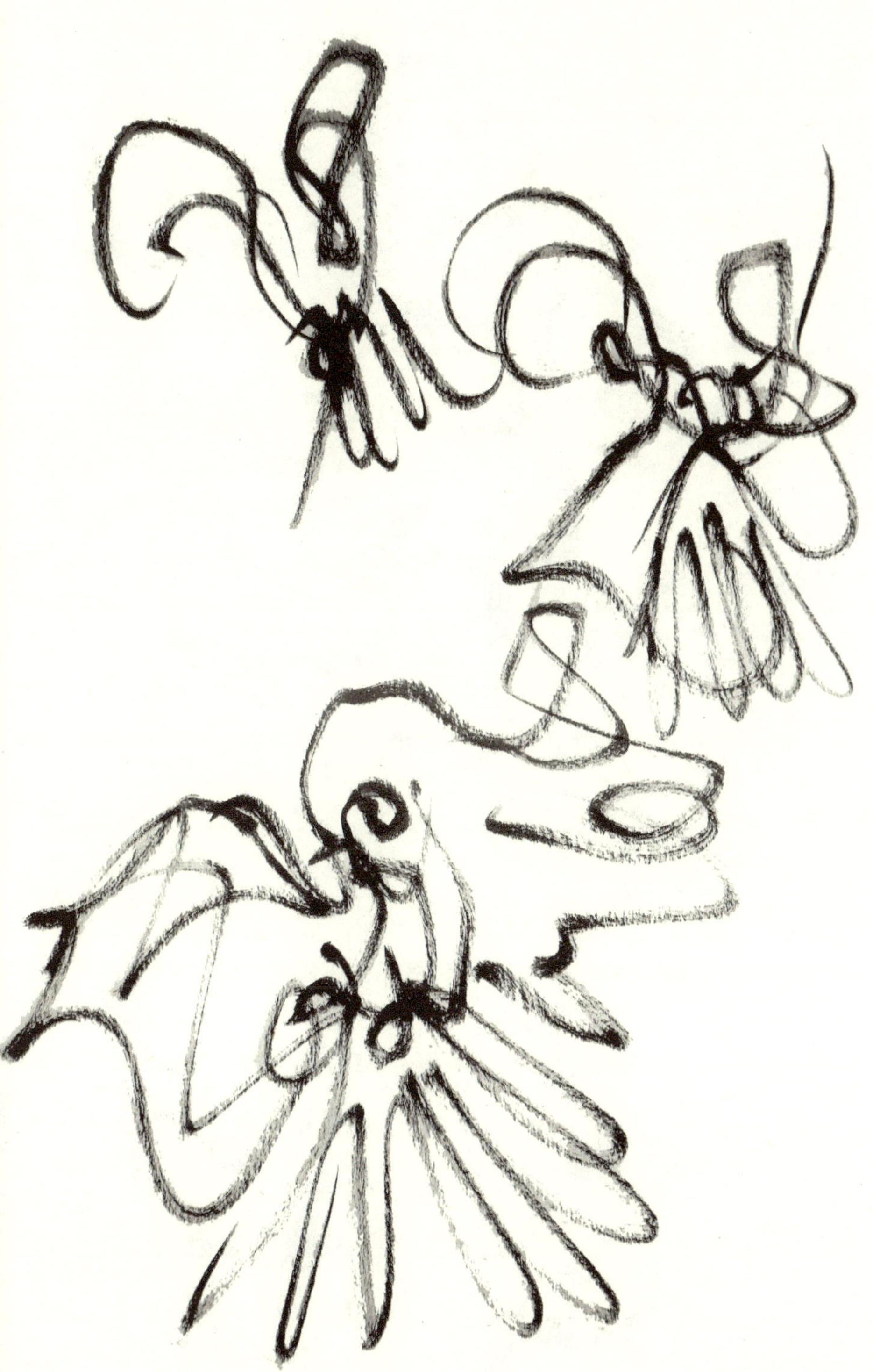

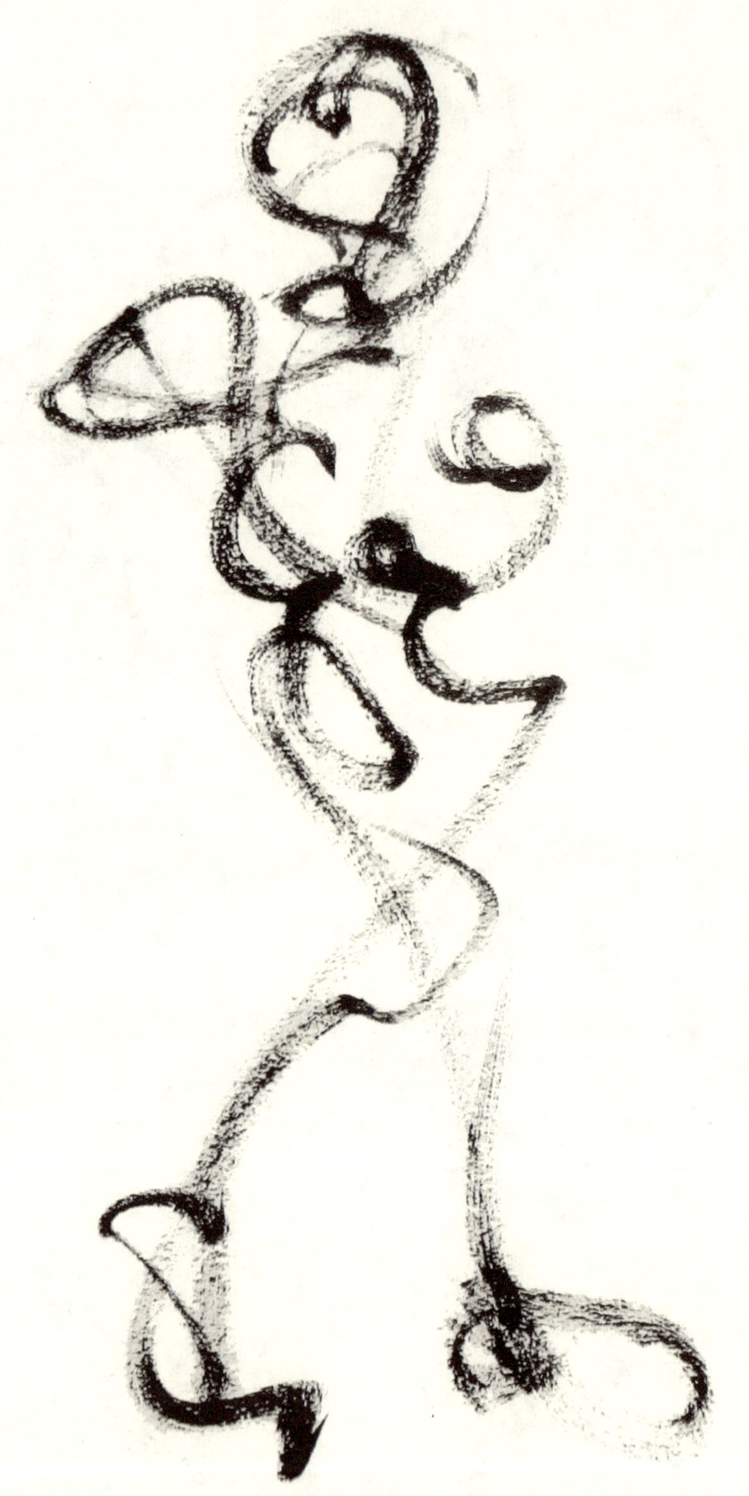

# Leblon-Ipanema-Copacabana: Rio de Janeiro

1

Blessed sand  form of glass  speckling clothes
insensate particle of time  you skirt
over the earth flitting  draping

O-cean  insatiate being  your salt waters divulge in our veins creatures
from the depths

The energy field around your lofty
mountains  accumulate over time  receiving sun's rays

Trees  miraculous lush—beacon of greenlight
purespirit  cathedral
of sounds   august  ethereal mindstrings

Eyelashes  lips  earth  mountains of breasts   valleys of buttocks
magnificent g-strings
entrusting all to look

Sun  lifegiver  entreat us to love
the earth as we all should

2

*Rio* the river a name for a city mistakenly named is tender
as a lover in the mornings

How to find again the names of places visited never revisited?
How to shovel away at our lives to find the smallest particle
representative of the whole what is dearest?

Backs to sand we listen to dreams & nightmares
the smells of ocean sand &
sex at the beach
samba heart beating bodies
pulsating gyrating
such delirious happiness
*Cariocas* cavort in preparation for Carnaval
Samba music carries hips & buttocks throbbing at nanoseconds
feasting
on lyrics & sweaty skin one another's
touch beat within the beat musicians bleating throbbing
blowing strumming

3

So many colors under the sun so many suns: Portuguese
moonskin potatochipskin mulatto skin black skin
& the world
sees itself a mosaic of flaming rain
*Garota de Ipanema* a cheap joint where artists sit & drink
to death
next to hills that jut into air
of mist & men & women running

4

Not of this earth luminous both dead & alive
closest to the gods to God crosses borders walking on water
a life led in many places
simultaneously

## The Imperial Palace

Tokyo

fish stroking
the edges of the world
little fetishes adorn cell phones
transmitting messages mundane
joyful & suicidal

in autumn  the Imperial Palace robes itself in yellow & red
trees     while evergreens
roam its slopes

along the moat  marathon
runners gallop
their muscles chiseled
by their motions

the most regal month red & yellow leaves enflame
the grounds
living in one time zone permits us to see the praying
mantis                climbing slowly stately
the *little bitty boy*
& his green scooter left crying

wild dogs on the hunt fierce as an arrow

the Crown Princess sits &

sighs from her window

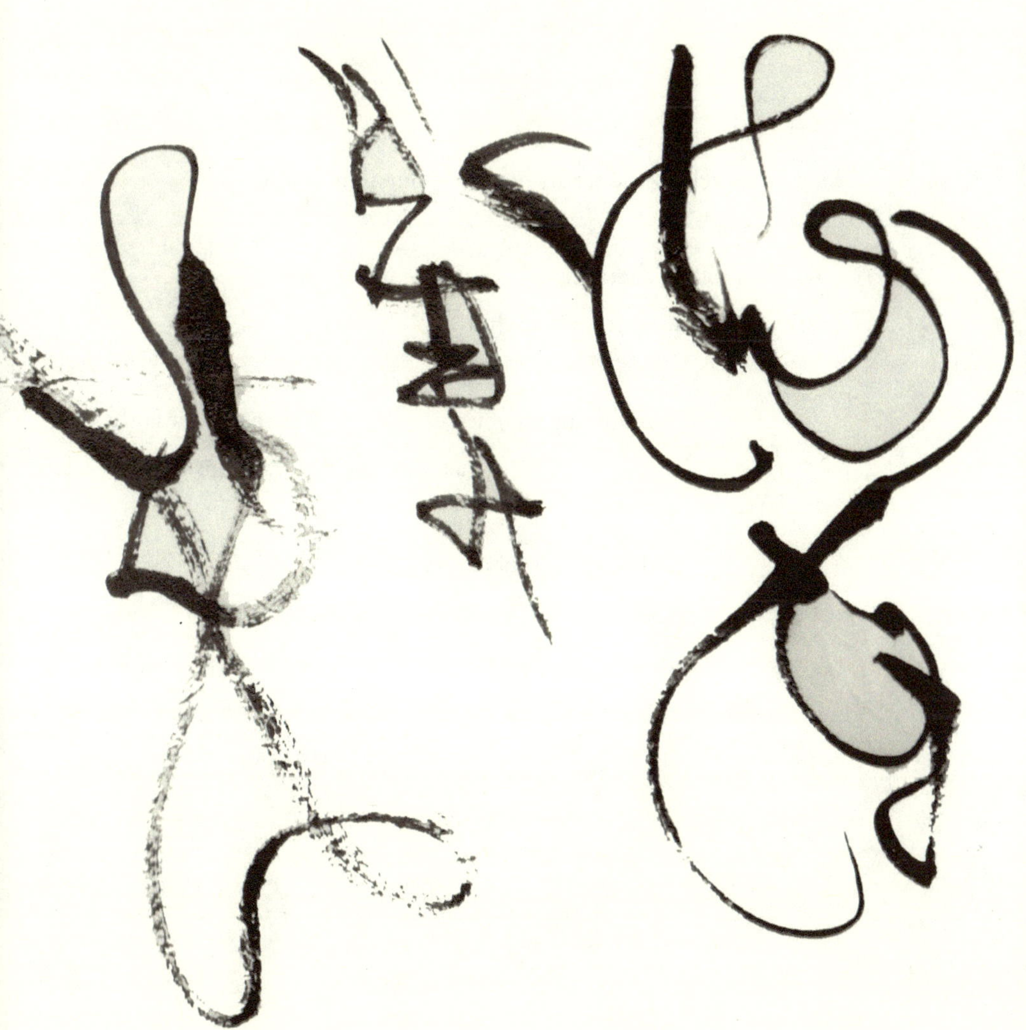

## Love Poem to Cherry Blossoms

kisses     rosy
inundating
your labium

trunks arching deliver their generous sermons

blossoms swelling the earth's bosom     bursting

a row of cherry trees          every one of you
every petal snowing from branches

blooming you bless                    legions to our faith
a moment   a largess translucent

in the snow of cherry
blossoms

[Tokyo 2003-2005]

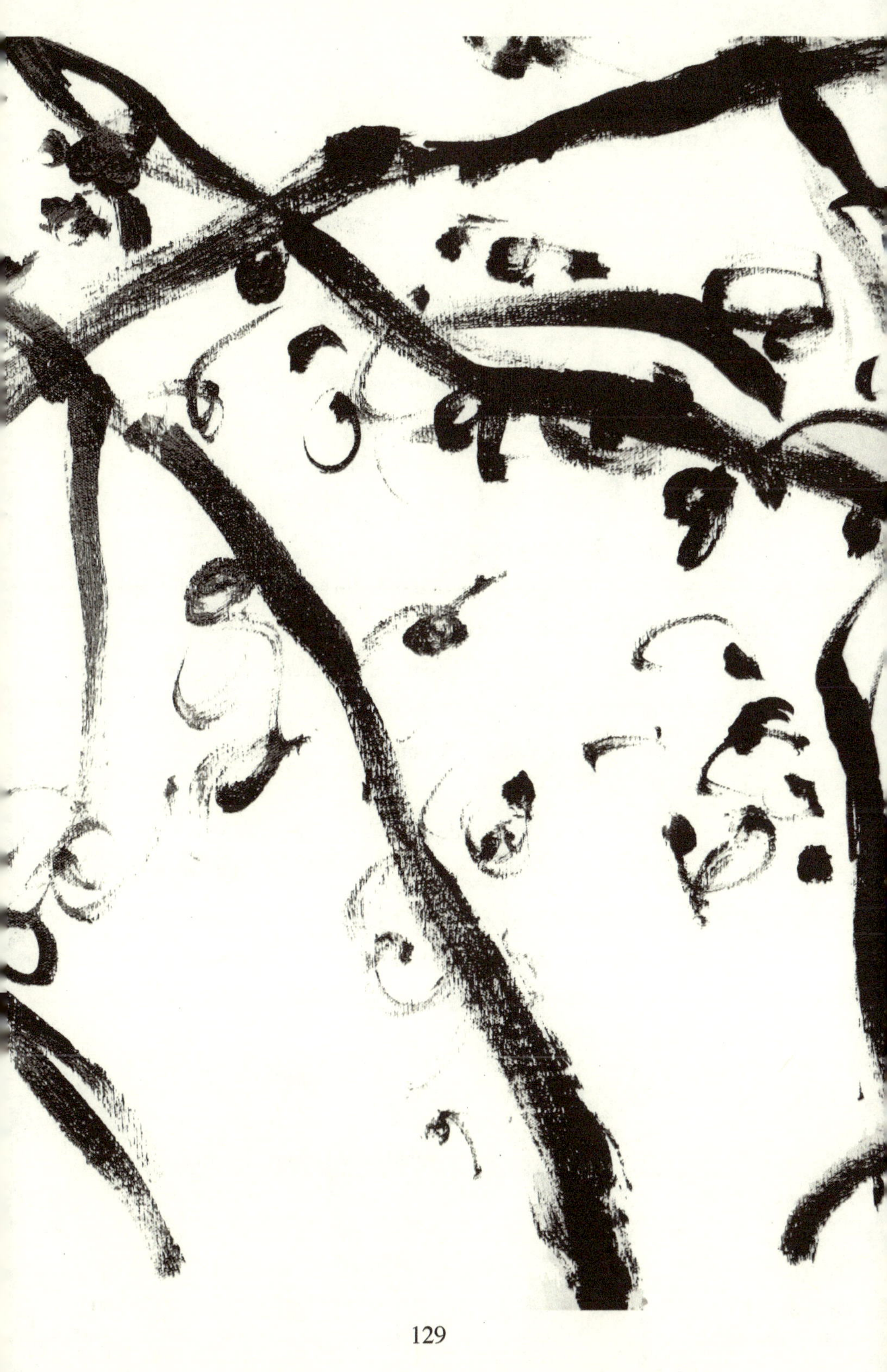

## A bird of laughing feathers

A song gregarious

Concord to every cell & mitochondrion
to every person all bodies nations
neighbors   sons daughters
brothers & sisters
of every skin color
to those who breathe  those who sleep
to those who kick & bother to dream
to those who dream   & die dreaming

Armistice to those with knives  guns & bombs

a nail   a grenade on one's back        cactus  scorched
a board   of thorns ashes

knocking                knocking

to those who die
fighting
limbs burned off eyes torched

to those who are alive

fighting  limbs bombed off   heart beating

A century in the forest

meditating under a tree

Repose to those with mercurial hearts

ailing

Peace to nocturnal invasions

bodily invasions

to the seers         the blind   & decrepit

To the pallbearers

a flowing river of blossoms

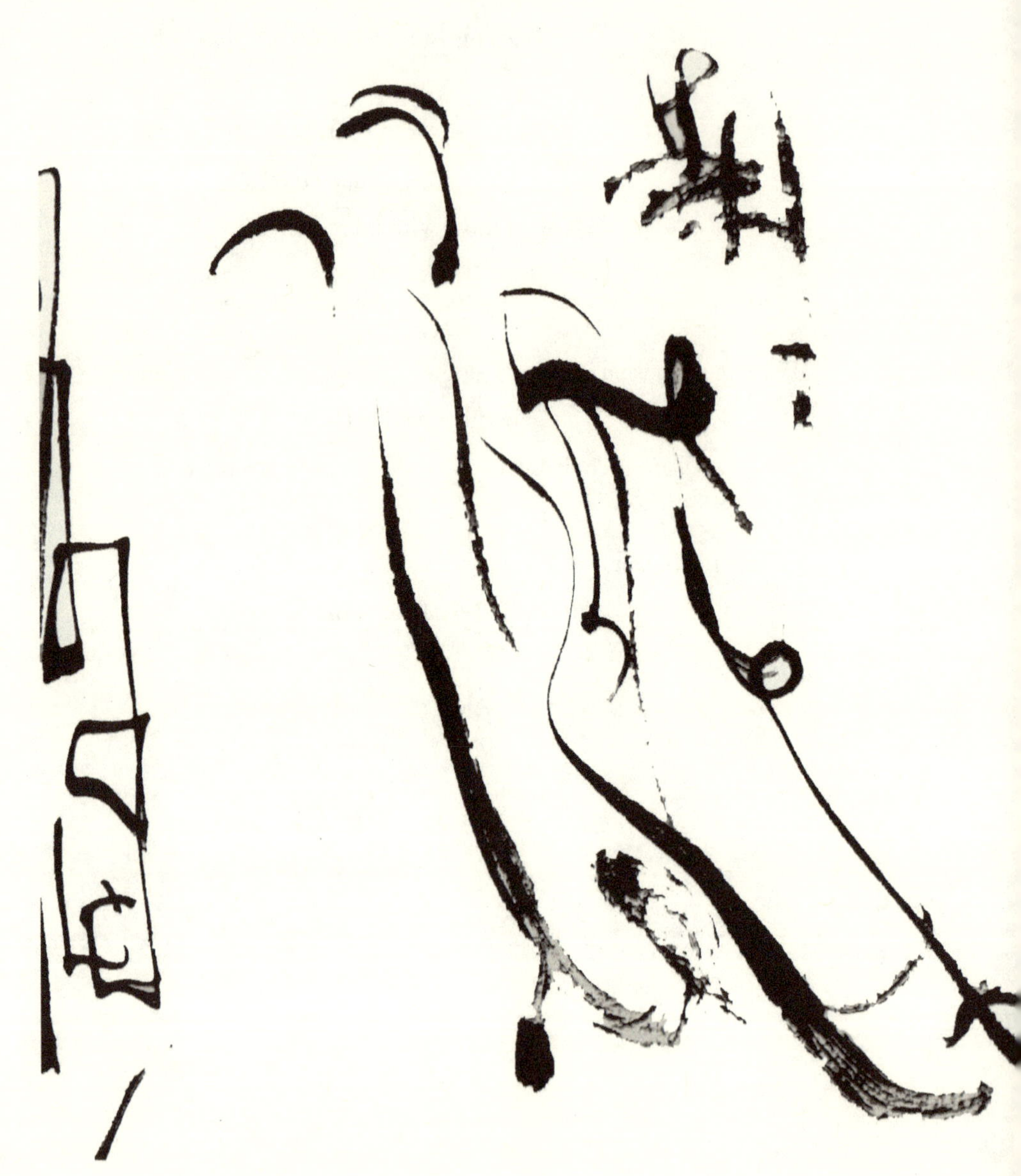

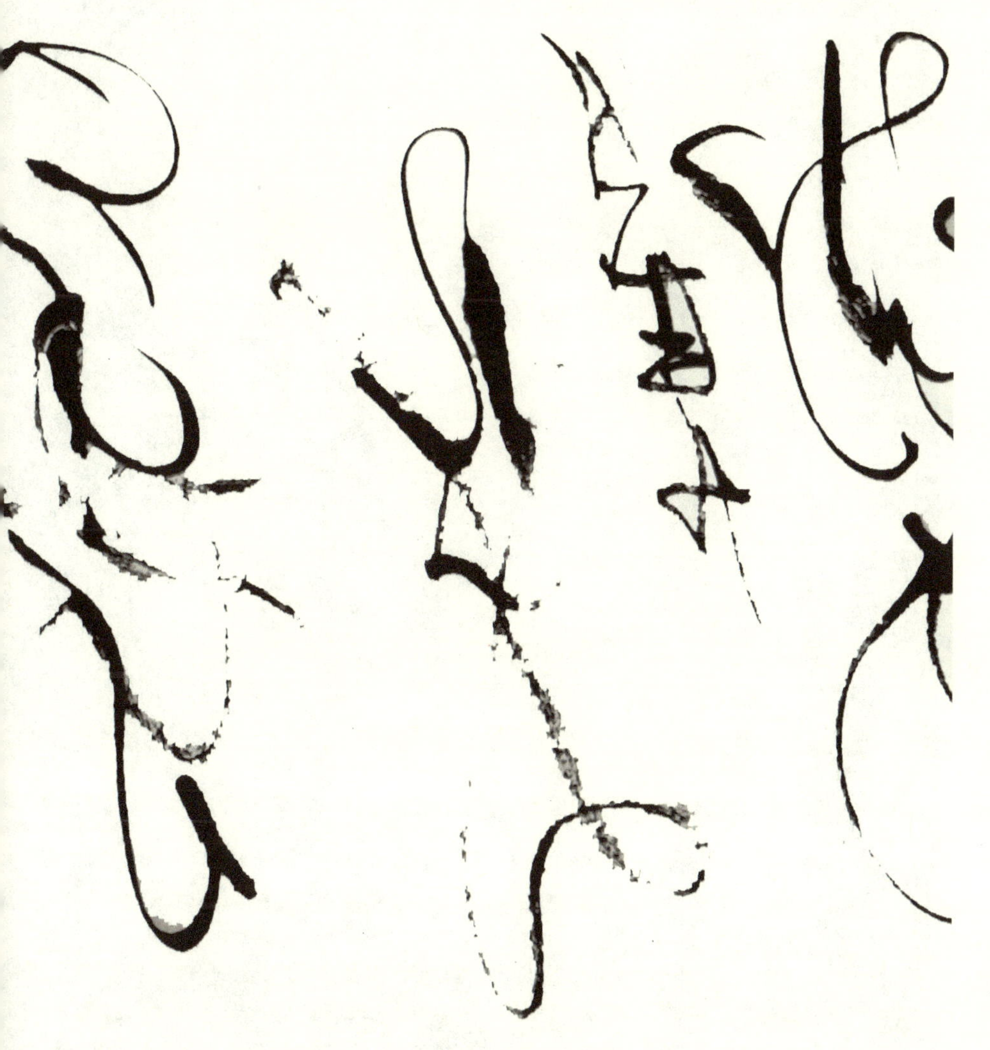

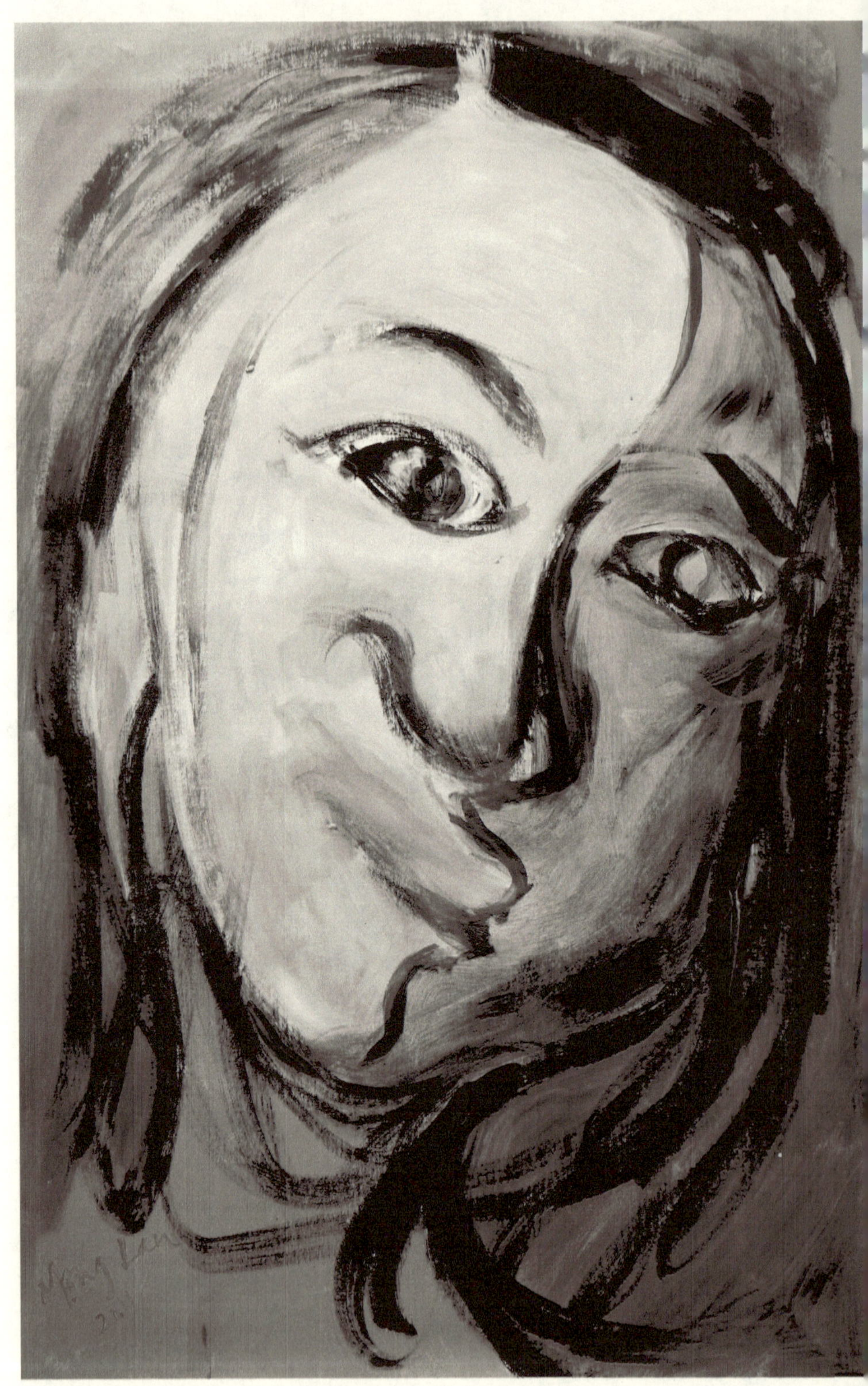

# BIOGRAPHY

Mộng-Lan, Vietnamese-born American artist, poet, writer, painter, photographer, Argentine tango dancer, singer, and educator, left her native Vietnam on the last day of the evacuation of Saigon. Winner of a Pushcart Prize, the Juniper Prize, the Great Lakes Colleges Association's New Writers Awards for Poetry, and other awards, Mộng-Lan's poetry has been nationally and internationally anthologized to include being in *Best American Poetry* and *The Pushcart Book of Poetry: Best Poems from 30 Years of the Pushcart Prize.* Author of seven previous books and chapbooks, Mộng-Lan's books include *Song of the Cicadas; Why is the Edge Always Windy?, Tango, Tangoing: Poems & Art; Tango, Tangueando: Poemas & Dibujos* (the bilingual Spanish-English edition); *Force of the Heart: Tango, Art; Love Poem to Tofu & Other Poems* (poetry & calligraphic art, chapbook); *Love Poem to Ginger & Other Poems: poetry & paintings* (chapbook).

A Stegner Fellow in poetry at Stanford University for two years and a Fulbright Fellow in Vietnam, Mộng-Lan took her Master of Fine Arts in creative writing at the University of Arizona. She won scholarships to study painting and the visual arts at the Glassell School of Art in Houston and at Schreiner College. Subsequently, her paintings and photographs have been exhibited for one year in the Capitol House in Washington D.C., in galleries and museums such as the Dallas Museum of Art, the Museum of Fine Arts in Houston, and in public exhibitions in Tokyo, Seoul, Bali, Bangkok, and Buenos Aires. In conjunction with a grant from the National Endowment for the Arts, she was the Dallas Museum of Fine Arts' inaugural Visual Artist and Poet in Residence in 2005. An exhibition of her paintings and photographs, "The World of Mộng-Lan," ran for six months.

Mộng-Lan has taught at the the University of Maryland in Tokyo, University of Arizona, and Stanford University. She also has given scores of readings and academic presentations in the United States, Argentina, Germany, Indonesia, Japan, Korea, Malaysia, Switzerland, Thailand, and Vietnam. Mộng-Lan travels frequently to give performances, readings and lectures, teach, show her artwork, and dance tango. She divides her time between the United States and Argentina. Visit: www.monglan.com

# NOTES

All paintings, drawings, and photographs are the work of Mộng-Lan.

pp. ii-iii, *Man & Beast*, pen & ink on rice paper, 2014.

p. v, *Orchid of the Imagination,* pen & ink on rice paper, 2014.

p. 1, *Explosion*, pen & ink on rice paper, 2014.

p. 5, *Handful of Fumes*, pen & ink on rice paper, 2014.

p. 6, *Woman Reclining Under Tree*, pen & ink on rice paper, 2014.

p.12, *Man Standing Under Tree*, pen & ink on rice paper, 2014.

p. 14, *Bình An* means "peace" in Vietnamese.

p. 18, *Circle of Memory*, pen & ink on paper, 2014.

pp. 24-25, *Galveston Beach Calm*, digital photograph, 2012.

p. 29, *Star Orchid*, pen & ink on rice paper, 2014.

p. 32, *Chili Peppers*, acrylic on canvas, 16 x 20 in (40 x 50 cm), 2007.

p. 34, *Spinach Leaf*, pen & ink on paper, 2007.

p. 36, *Bánh cuốn* (rice flour steamed rolls) is a northern Vietnamese dish, hailing from Thanh Trì district just outside Hà Nội. Minced pork, mushrooms and prawns are wrapped in a flimsy rice film. It comes served with sliced cucumber, *chả lụa*, beansprouts, sprinkled with deep-fried shallots and chopped mint with a *nước mắm* (fish sauce) dip.

p. 37, *Bánh Cuốn*, pen & ink on paper, 2007.

p. 38, *Bún Riêu* is a crabmeat noodle soup, from Northern Vietnam.

p. 44, *Love Poem to Phở*, acrylic on canvas, 16 x 20 in (40 x 50 cm), 2007.

p. 47, *Briskly*, pen & ink on paper, 2007.

p. 55, *Moon & River*, pen & ink on paper, 2007.

p. 58, *Reclining Figure*, pen & ink on paper, 2007.

p. 59, The poem, "Sentient Figure," based on a sculpture of the same name in its permanent collection, was commissioned by the Dallas Museum of Art. In 2005, Mộng-Lan was the Museum's Inaugural Poet and Visual Artist in Residence. For six months, her paintings and photographs were exhibited in the Museum in an exhibition entitled, "The World of Mộng-Lan."

p. 61, *Fugue & Wave*, pen & ink on paper, 2006.

p. 62, *Navigation*, pen & ink on paper, 2006.

p. 65, *Hallucination with Clay*, pen & ink on paper, 2007.

p. 72, *Nonchalant Luster*, pen & ink on paper, 2007.

p. 74, *Mountains, Coyotes'* tongues, pen & ink on paper, 2007.

p. 81, *Earth's Iridescent Skirt*, pen & ink on paper, 2007.

p. 84, *Bombers*, pen & ink on paper, 2007.

pp. 90-91, *Cherry Blossoms*, acrylic on canvas, 27 x 39 in (70 x 100 cm), 2012.

p. 95, *Café au Lait*, pen & ink on rice paper, 2007.

p. 99, *Love Poem to Garlic*, mixed media on canvas, 16 x 20 in (40 x 50 cm), 2012.

p. 100, *Basil Leaf*, acrylic on canvas, 2012.

p. 102, *Onion*, pen & ink on paper, 11 x 14 in (28 x 35 cm), 2007.

p. 105, *Ginger & Basil*, detail, acrylic on canvas, 27 x 39 in (70 x 100 cm), 2012.

p. 106, *Lemons & Leeks*, detail, acrylic on canvas, 27 x 39 in (70 x 100 cm), 2012.

p. 110, *Soto* is Indonesia's national dish, a traditional soup composed of broth, meat and vegetables. The ingredients of *soto* vary from region to region in Indonesia.

p. 112, *A School of Fish Ascending*, acrylic on canvas, 27 x 39 in (70 x 100 cm), 2012.

pp. 114-115, *Smoky Cities*, pen & ink on rice paper, 2014.

p. 121, *Palomas*, 9.5 x 12.5 in (24 x 32 cm), pen & ink on paper, 2012.

p. 122, *Persona,* 11 x 14 in (28 x 35 cm), pen & ink on paper, 2011.

p. 127, *Crown Princess*, pen & ink on rice paper, 2014.

p. 129, *Cherry Blossoms*, detail, acrylic on canvas, 27 x 39 in (70 x 100 cm), 2012.

pp. 132-133, *Procession of Thoughts,* pen & ink on rice paper, 2014.

p. 134, *Face of Duality*, acrylic on canvas, 27 x 39 in (70 x 100 cm), 2012.

p. 139, *Three Women in Society*, pen & ink on rice paper, 2014.

p. 142, *Tango Dancers*, pen & ink on paper, 2012.

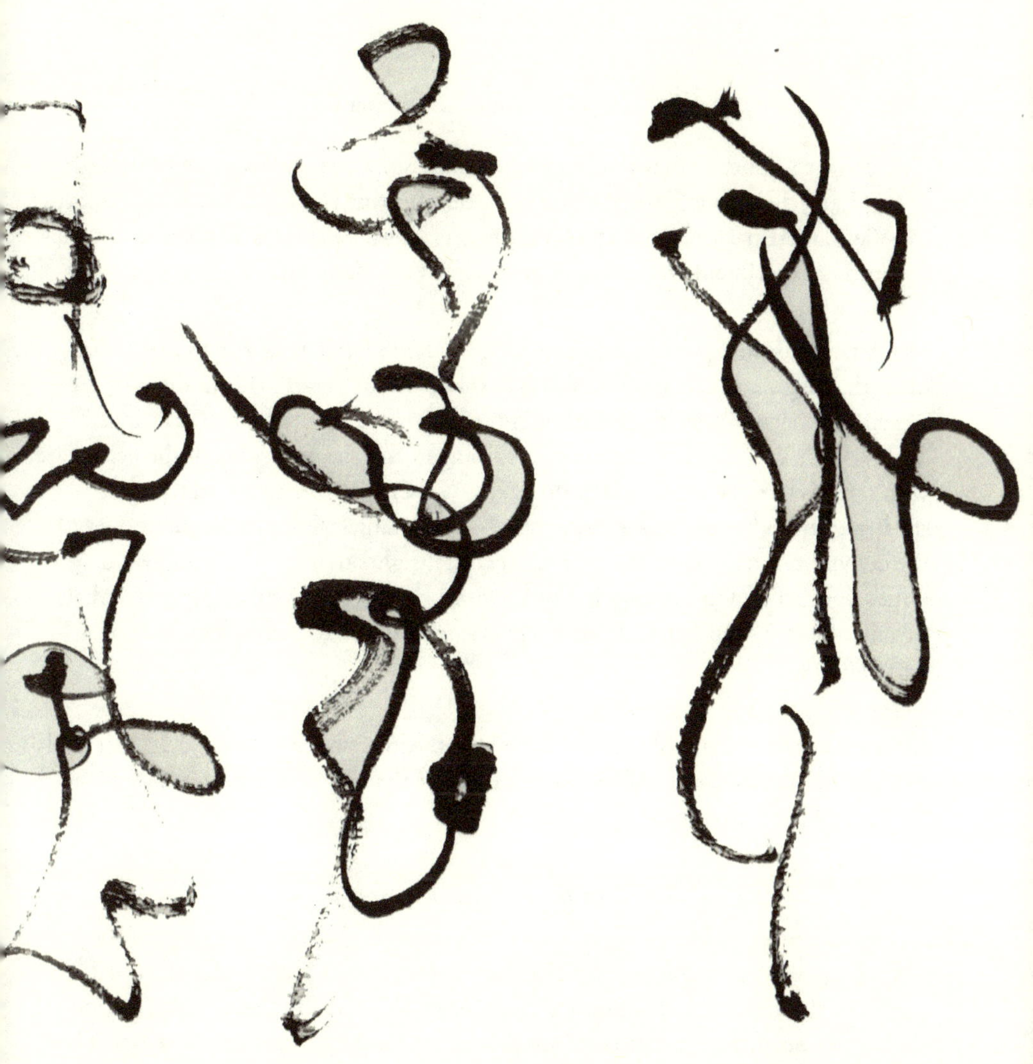

## Praise for Mộng-Lan's books:

On *Song of the Cicadas* (Juniper Prize)

"Welcome to a poetic voice that represents no less than a manifestation of soul. In Mộng-Lan's debut book, she has taken on the daunting responsibility of representing the Vietnamese nation and culture, via imagery, consciousness, and memory. Hers is a stunning experiment and a historical imperative."—Jane Miller

" In Asian tradition, poetry and visual art go hand in hand, with the collaboration of work, image, and calligraphy. Mộng-Lan's first book renews this tradition for American poetry, and with a startling subject matter. Her poems and drawings dealing with Viet Nam reflect the awe, the anger, and the mourning of the expatriate who returns to the country of her birth . . . . We sense that she also values what she brings from her own adoptive culture—a new language, a new aesthetic, and the conviction that a woman artist has special insights to offer on the subject of armed conflict and its aftermath. From visual beauty, human suffering, and verbal inventiveness, Mộng-Lan stakes out a poetic territory that is completely her own."—Alfred Corn

"Mộng-Lan is a remarkably accomplished poet. Always her poems are deft, extremely graceful in the way words move, and the cadence that carries them . . . . Clearly she is a master of the art."—Robert Creeley

On *Why Is The Edge Always Windy?*

" 'what you've lived through    you are,' says Mộng-Lan in 'Coast,' one of the early poems in this beautiful, spellbinding book, *Why Is The Edge Always Windy?* One should not be mislead by the title into thinking Mộng-Lan's work will be airy. The lyricism of her writing sings not of the ethereal but of a hard land; her work speaks not of arrested moments but of the tectonic force of history, which, moving at the pace of geological time, presses cultures against each other, folds moments over each other, edges everywhere and always exposed. Indeed, Mộng-Lan's are poems of exposure. Reading them is revelatory."—Lyn Hejinian

"Mộng-Lan 's *Why Is The Edge Always Windy?* is a stunning book that turns our "era of exile" into one of lyric possession, the impulses to lament and to praise whirling together into a bittersweet music. I'm amazed at how these poems hold the complexity and contradiction of a global world view that spans from Hanoi to New York, from Chiapas to San Francisco, while still striking notes of intimacy and making formally beautiful sense."—Alison Hawthorne Deming

On *Tango, Tangoing: Poems & Art*

"A mesmerizing accomplishment—four voices at their climax: the dance, if we can call it that, the physics of being, the history and manual of dark beauty and the *voleos* of line, ink, stanza and voice, layers of loss, desire and the body in ecstatic explosions. Three drops of Lorca, one tincture of María Luisa Bombal and a full vasija of Mộng-Lan, a masterpiece, señores y señoras. A mathematics of fire."—Juan Felipe Herrera

"While the ostensible subject here is dance, Mộng-Lan is brilliant at suggesting layered, ever-shifting perspectives, meanings, and voices. These complex poems are, at times, aesthetic mediations, dissections of human relationships, internal monologues, and political inquiry. That Mộng-Lan succeeds at such an ambitious project in writing that is visually striking, musically complex, unabashedly erotic and deeply intelligent, is testimony to her very great poetic talents. This is a marvelous book, one I'll return to again and again."—Kevin Prufer

"Mộng-Lan's lyric poetry is unlike any others. The work sings, but it is not music alone that moves us; it's what we experience through the speaker's observational accuracy and emotional wisdom: 'The oscillatory / foolish / the insane / make their way / into tangos' and 'I would find you / locked in a mosquito's eye.' Consisting of three extraordinary poems about Argentine tango, the work is '*muy generoso*,' as she quotes the dance itself as being, in its sweep and precision. The poems are not merely illustrative of the dance's famous forwardness; they reveal the transformative power of the commitment the dance requires: the finding of rhythm with another at the edge of mayhem, even as stillness is created at the center of the *ochos*, emblems of infinity, the dancers create on the floor." —Paul Hoover

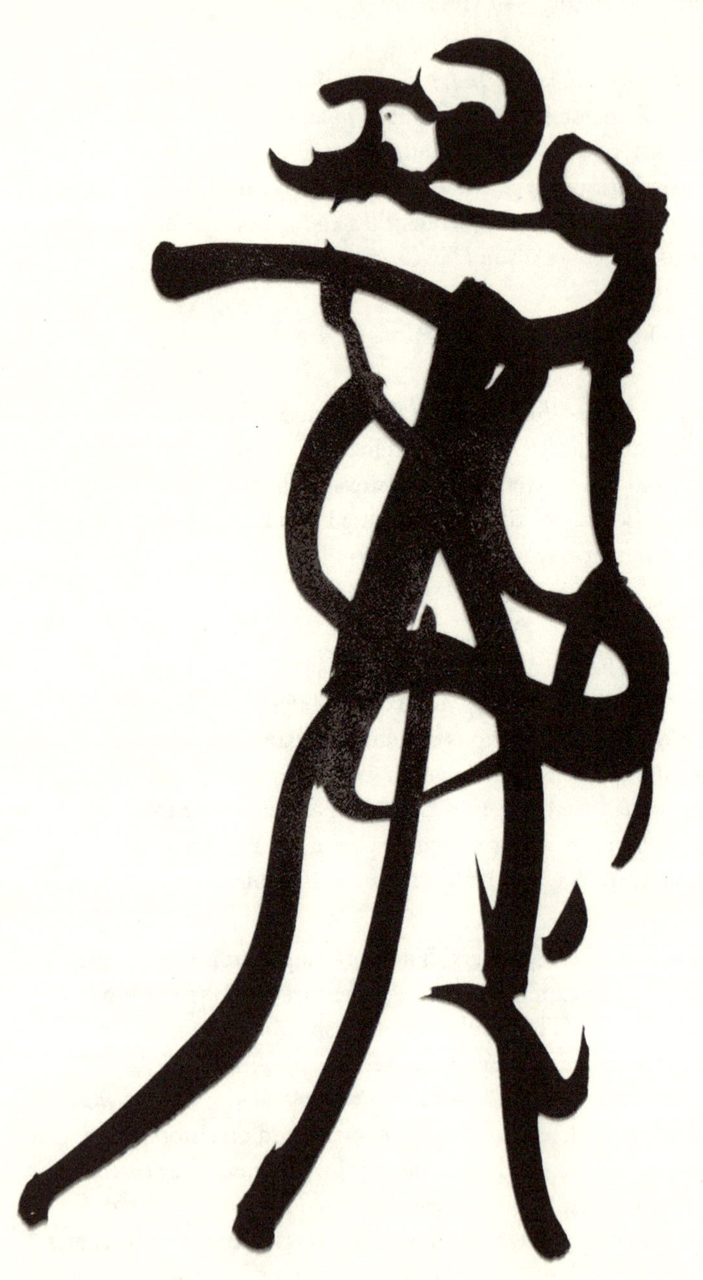
Ming Lau 2012

www.ingramcontent.com/pod-product-compliance
Lightning Source LLC
LaVergne TN
LVHW090957080826
845145LV00003B/1033

* 9 7 8 0 9 8 2 8 2 2 7 2 2 *